SMALL BUSINESS ASSISTANCE

TRAINING AND INVESTMENT PROGRAMS

Business Economics in a Rapidly-Changing World

Additional books in this series can be found on Nova's website under the Series tab.

Additional E-books in this series can be found on Nova's website under the E-book tab.

Business Issues, Competition and Entrepreneurship

Additional books in this series can be found on Nova's website under the Series tab.

Additional E-books in this series can be found on Nova's website under the E-book tab.

BUSINESS ECONOMICS IN A RAPIDLY-CHANGING WORLD

SMALL BUSINESS ASSISTANCE

TRAINING AND INVESTMENT PROGRAMS

Patrick J. Walker

EDITOR

Nova Science Publishers, Inc.

New York

For permission to use material from this book please contact us:
Telephone 631-231-7269; Fax 631-231-8175
Web Site: http://www.novapublishers.com

Library of Congress Cataloging-in-Publication Data

Small business assistance : training and investment programs / editor, Patrick J. Walker.
    p. cm.
  Includes index.
  ISBN 978-1-62100-707-4 (softcover)
  1. Small business--United States. 2. Small business--United States--Management. 3. Small business--United State--Finance. 4. United States. Small Business Administration. I. Walker, Patrick J.
  HD2346.U5S6126 2011
  354.2'7990973--dc23
                          2011037429

Published by Nova Science Publishers, Inc. † New York

CONTENTS

PREFACE

The Small Business Administration (SBA) has provided "technical and managerial aides to small-business concerns, by advising and counseling on matters in connection with government procurement and on policies, principles and practices of good management" since it began operations in 1953. Initially, the SBA provided its own small business management and technical assistance training programs. However, over time, the SBA has relied increasingly on third parties to provide that training. This new book examines the historical development of federal small business management and technical assistance training programs; describes their current structures, operations, and budgets and assesses their administration and oversight, and the measures used to determine their effectiveness.

Chapter 1- The Small Business Administration (SBA) has provided "technical and managerial aides to small-business concerns, by advising and counseling on matters in connection with government procurement and on policies, principles and practices of good management" since it began operations in 1953. Initially, the SBA provided its own small business management and technical assistance training programs. However, over time, the SBA has relied increasingly on third parties to provide that training.

In FY2010, the SBA provided $239 million in funding to about "14,000 resource partners," including about 1,000 small business development centers, 110 women's business centers, and 364 chapters of the mentoring program, SCORE. The SBA reports that about 1.1 million aspiring entrepreneurs and small business owners received training from an SBA-supported resource partner in FY2010. The SBA has argued that these programs contribute "to the long-term success of these businesses and their ability to grow and create jobs."

Chapter 2- The Small Business Administration (SBA) administers several programs to support small businesses, including loan guaranty programs to enhance small business access to capital; programs to increase small business opportunities in federal contracting; direct loans for businesses, homeowners, and renters to assist their recovery from natural disasters; and access to entrepreneurial education to assist with business formation and expansion. It also administers the Small Business Investment Company (SBIC) Program. Authorized by P.L. 85-699, the Small Business Investment Act of 1958, as amended, the SBIC program enhances small business access to venture capital by stimulating and supplementing "the flow of private equity capital and long term loan funds which small business concerns need for the sound financing of their business operations and for their growth, expansion, and modernization, and which are not available in adequate supply." Facilitating the flow of capital to small businesses to stimulate the national economy was, and remains, the SBIC program's primary objective.

The SBA does not make direct investments in small businesses. It works with 302 privately owned and managed SBICs licensed by the SBA to provide financing to small businesses with private capital the SBIC has raised and with funds the SBIC borrows at favorable rates because the SBA guarantees the debenture (loan obligation).

In: Small Business Assistance
Editors: Patrick J. Walker

ISBN: 978-1-62100- 707-4
© 2012 Nova Science Publishers, Inc.

Chapter 1

SMALL BUSINESS MANAGEMENT AND TECHNICAL ASSISTANCE TRAINING PROGRAMS

Robert Jay Dilger and Oscar R. Gonzales

SUMMARY

The Small Business Administration (SBA) has provided "technical and managerial aides to small-business concerns, by advising and counseling on matters in connection with government procurement and on policies, principles and practices of good management" since it began operations in 1953. Initially, the SBA provided its own small business management and technical assistance training programs. However, over time, the SBA has relied increasingly on third parties to provide that training.

In FY2010, the SBA provided $239 million in funding to about "14,000 resource partners," including about 1,000 small business development centers, 110 women's business centers, and 364 chapters of the mentoring program, SCORE. The SBA reports that about 1.1 million aspiring entrepreneurs and small business owners received training from an SBA-supported resource partner in FY2010. The SBA has argued that these programs contribute "to the long-term success of these businesses and their ability to grow and create jobs."

Table 1. SBA Management and Technical Assistance Training Programs Funding

Training Program	FY2010
Small Business Development Center Grants Program	$129,428,000
Women's Business Center Grants Program	$23,525,000
Microloan Technical Assistance Program	$22,556,000
Entrepreneurial Development Initiatives (clusters)	$12,451,000
SCORE (Service Corps of Retired Executives)	$11,135,000
PRIME Technical Assistance Program	$8,108,000
Veterans Business Development Program	$7,644,000
7(j) Technical Assistance Program	$6,580,000
Native American Outreach Program	$4,050,000
Other Training Programs	$13,684,000
Total	$239,161,000

Source: U.S. Small Business Administration, *Agency Financial Report, Fiscal Year 2010* (Washington, DC: GPO, 2010), p. 83; and U.S. Small Business Administration, Office of Congressional and Legislative Affairs, correspondence with the author, January 19, 2011.

The Department of Commerce also provides management and technical assistance training for small businesses. For example, its Minority Business Development Agency provides training to minority business owners to assist them in becoming suppliers to private corporations and the federal government.

A recurring theme at congressional hearings concerning the SBA's management and technical assistance training programs has been the perceived need to improve program efficiency by eliminating duplication of services and increasing cooperation and coordination both within and among SCORE, women's business centers (WBCs), and small business development centers (SBDCs). For example, on March 15, 2011, the House Committee on Small Business recommended that several SBA training programs be defunded "because they duplicate existing programs at the SBA or at other agencies." Congress has also explored ways to improve the SBA's measurement of the programs' effectiveness and to address the impact of national economic conditions on WBC and SBDC finances and their capacity to maintain client service levels and meet federal matching requirements.

This report examines the historical development of federal small business management and technical assistance training programs; describes their current structures, operations, and budgets; and assesses their administration and oversight, the measures used to determine their effectiveness, and WBC and SBDC finances and their capacity to maintain client service levels and meet federal matching requirements.

This report also discusses P.L. 111-240, the Small Business Jobs Act of 2010. It authorizes $50 million in additional funds for SBDCs to provide targeted technical assistance to small businesses for various specified activities, such as seeking access to capital or credit; guarantees each state not less than $325,000 of these additional funds; and waives the non-federal matching requirement for these funds. The act also authorizes the SBA to temporarily waive, in whole or in part, for successive fiscal years, the non-federal share matching requirement relating to "technical assistance and counseling" for WBCs. Two bills introduced during the 111th Congress, H.R. 2352, the Job Creation Through Entrepreneurship Act of 2009, and S. 3967, the Small Business Investment and Innovation Act of 2010, are also examined. They would authorize several changes to the SBA's management and technical assistance training programs in an effort to improve their performance and oversight.

FEDERAL MANAGEMENT AND TECHNICAL ASSISTANCE TRAINING PROGRAMS

The Small Business Administration (SBA) administers several programs to support small businesses, including loan guaranty programs to enhance small business access to capital; programs to increase small business opportunities in federal contracting; direct loans for businesses, homeowners, and renters to assist their recovery from natural disasters; and access to entrepreneurial education to assist with business formation and expansion.[1] The SBA has provided "technical and managerial aides to small-business concerns, by advising and counseling on matters in connection with government procurement and on policies, principles and practices of good management" since it began operations in 1953.[2]

Initially, the SBA provided its own management and technical assistance training programs. However, over time, the SBA has relied increasingly on third parties to provide that training.

In FY2010, the SBA provided more than $239 million for third-party management and technical assistance training for small businesses (see Table

1). More than 1.1 million aspiring entrepreneurs and small business owners received training from an SBA-supported resource partner in FY2010.[3]

The SBA has argued that its support of management and technical assistance training for small businesses has contributed "to the long-term success of these businesses and their ability to grow and create jobs."[4] It currently provides financial support to about "14,000 resource partners," including about 1,000 small business development centers (SBDCs), 110 women's business centers (WBCs), and 364 chapters of the mentoring program, SCORE.[5]

The Department of Commerce also provides management and technical assistance training for small businesses. For example, the Department of Commerce's Minority Business Development Agency provides training to minority business owners to assist them in becoming suppliers to private corporations and the federal government.[6] In addition, the Department of Commerce's Economic Development Administration's Local Technical Assistance Program promotes efforts to build and expand local organizational capacity in economically distressed areas. As part of that effort, it funds projects that focus on technical or market feasibility studies of economic development projects or programs, which often include consultation with small businesses.[7]

For many years, a recurring theme at congressional hearings concerning the SBA's management and technical assistance training programs has been the perceived need to improve program efficiency by eliminating duplication of services and increasing cooperation and coordination both within and among its training resource partners. For example, on March 15, 2011, the House Committee on Small Business recommended to the House Committee on the Budget that several SBA management and technical assistance training programs be defunded, including funding for WBCs, "because they duplicate existing programs at the SBA or at other agencies."[8]

Congress has also explored ways to improve the SBA's measurement of the programs' effectiveness and to address the impact of national economic conditions on WBC and SBDC finances and their capacity to meet federal matching requirements and to maintain client service levels.

This report examines the historical development of federal small business management and technical assistance training programs; describes their current structures, operations, and budgets; and assesses their administration and oversight, the measures used to determine their effectiveness, and WBC and SBDC finances and their capacity to maintain client service levels and meet federal matching requirements.

This report discusses P.L. 111-240, the Small Business Jobs Act of 2010. It authorizes $50 million in additional funds for SBDCs to provide targeted technical assistance to small businesses for various specified activities, such as seeking access to capital or credit, federal procurement opportunities, and opportunities to export products. The act also guarantees each state not less than $325,000 of these additional funds and waives the non-federal matching requirement for these additional funds.

This report also discusses two bills introduced during the 111th Congress: H.R. 2352, the Job Creation Through Entrepreneurship Act of 2009, and S. 3967, the Small Business Investment and Innovation Act of 2010. They would authorize several changes to these programs in an effort to improve their performance and oversight.

SBA MANAGEMENT AND TECHNICAL ASSISTANCE TRAINING PROGRAMS

The SBA supports a number of management and technical assistance training programs, including the

- Small Business Development Center Grants Program,
- Women's Business Center Grants Program,
- Microloan Technical Assistance Program,
- SCORE (Service Corps of Retired Executives),
- PRIME Technical Assistance Program,
- Veterans Business Development Programs,
- 7(j) Technical Assistance Program, and
- Native American Outreach Program.

The legislative history and current operating structures, functions, and budget for each of these programs is presented. In addition, if the data are available, their performance based on outcome-based measures, such as their effect on small business formation, survivability, and expansion, and on job creation and retention, is also presented. Also, a brief description of each of these programs is provided in the Appendix.

Given that it has only recently become operational, the SBA Entrepreneurial Development Initiatives Program is not discussed in detail. It is designed to "accelerate small business opportunities in existing regional clusters across the country."[9] Regional clusters are "geographic concentrations of firms and industries that do business with each other and have common needs for talent, technology, and infrastructure."[10] Regional cluster advocates argue that these networks "create a multiplier effect that increases efficiency, innovation, and ultimately produces conditions for high-growth, high-impact small businesses to prosper."[11] The SBA's Entrepreneurial Development Initiatives Program will provide 15 one-year grants of up to $600,000 each, with an option for an additional funding year, to local and regional business clusters to "provide business training, commercialization and technology transfer services, counseling, mentoring and other services that support the growth and development of small businesses in the cluster area and its industries."[12] The first 10 grant awards, selected from 173 applicants, were announced on September 20, 2010.[13] The clusters "will be assessed on the impact they will have on the region's economic growth, creation of sustainable jobs and the opportunities the cluster provides for small businesses."[14]

Small Business Development Centers

In 1976, the SBA created the University Business Development Center pilot program to establish small business centers within universities to provide counseling and training for small businesses. The first center was founded at California State Polytechnic University at Pomona in December, 1976. Seven more centers were funded over the next six months at universities in seven different states. By 1979, 16 small business development centers (SBDCs) received SBA funding and were providing management and technical training assistance to small businesses.[15]

The SBDC program was given statutory authorization by P.L. 96-302, the Small Business Development Center Act of 1980.[16] SBDCs were to "rely on the private sector primarily, and the university community, in partnership with the SBA and its other programs, to fill gaps in making quality management assistance available to the small business owner."[17] Although most SBDCs continued to be affiliated with universities, the legislation authorized the SBA to provide funding

> to any State government or any agency thereof, any regional entity, any State-chartered development, credit or finance corporation, any public or private institution of higher education, including but not limited to any land-grant college or university, any college or school

of business, engineering, commerce, or agriculture, community college or junior college, or to any entity formed by two or more of the above entities.[18]

SBDC funding is allocated on a pro rata basis among the states (defined to include the District of Columbia, the Commonwealth of Puerto Rico, the Virgin Islands, Guam, and American Samoa) by a statutory formula "based on the percentage of the population of each State, as compared to the population of the United States."[19] If, as is currently the case, SBDC funding exceeds $90 million, the minimum funding level is "the sum of $500,000, plus a percentage of $500,000 equal to the percentage amount by which the amount made available exceeds $90 million."[20]

In 1984, P.L. 98-395, the Small Business Development Center Improvement Act of 1984, required SBDCs, as a condition of receiving SBA funding, to contribute a matching amount equal to the grant amount, and that the match must be provided by non-federal sources and be comprised of not less than 50% cash and not more than 50% of indirect costs and in-kind contributions.[21] It also required SBDCs to have an advisory board and a full-time director who has authority to make expenditures under the center's budget. It also required the SBA to implement a program of onsite evaluations for each SBDC and to make those evaluations at least once every two years.

Today, the SBA provides grants to SBDCs that are "hosted by leading universities, colleges, and state economic development agencies" to deliver management and technical assistance training "to small businesses and nascent entrepreneurs (pre-venture) in order to promote growth, expansion, innovation, increased productivity and management improvement."[22] These services are delivered, in most instances, on a non-fee, one-on-one confidential counseling basis and are administered by 63 lead service centers, one located in each state (four in Texas and six in California), the District of Columbia, Puerto Rico, the Virgin Islands, Guam and American Samoa.[23] These lead centers manage nearly 1,000 service centers located throughout the United States and the territories.[24]

The SBDC program assisted 209,558 small business owners and prospective owners in FY2010.[25] Its funding for FY2010 was $129.4 million.[26] In addition, P.L. 111-240, the Small Business Jobs Act of 2010, authorizes to be appropriated $50 million in additional funds for SBDCs to provide targeted technical assistance to small businesses for various specified activities, such as seeking access to capital or credit, federal procurement opportunities, and opportunities to export products. The act also guarantees each state not less than $325,000 of these additional funds and waives the non-federal matching requirement for these additional funds.[27]

Special areas of emphasis for the SBDC program include "technology transfer and other assistance to high growth companies, defense economic transition assistance, disaster recovery assistance, energy efficiency, veterans assistance, manufacturing, technology, international trade, and market research and development."[28] In FY2010, 13,639 new businesses were formed with assistance from SBDC counselors.[29]

As part of its legislative mandate to evaluate each SBDC, in 2003, the SBA's Office of Entrepreneurial Development designed "a multi-year time series study to assess the impact of the programs it offers to small businesses."[30] The survey has been administered annually by a private firm. The latest survey findings were released on September 13, 2010.

The latest survey was sent to 22,092 SBDC clients in 2009 to assess their "initial attitudinal assessment of their counseling experience, and a follow-up with 2007 and 2008 clients to assess the financial impact of the received assistance."[31] A total of 4,320 surveys were completed.[32]

The 2009 survey of SBDC clients indicated that

- approximately 76% of SBDC respondents reported that the information they received from their counselor was valuable,
- 74% of SBDC respondents that received between three and five hours and 79% that received more than five hours of counseling rated SBDC usefulness as "high" as compared to 74% of respondents that received less than three hours of counseling, and
- 35% of start-up clients and 39% of in-business clients reported that they were able to increase sales as a result of SBDC assistance.[33]

Women's Business Centers

The Women's Business Center (WBC) Renewable Grant Program was initially established by P.L. 100-533, the Women's Business Ownership Act of 1988, as the Women's Business Demonstration Pilot Program. The act directed the SBA to provide financial assistance to private, nonprofit organizations to conduct demonstration projects giving financial, management, and marketing assistance to small businesses, including start-up businesses, owned and controlled by women. Since its inception, the program has targeted the needs of socially and economically disadvantaged women.[34] The WBC program was expanded and provided permanent legislative status by P.L. 109-108, the Science, State, Justice, Commerce, and Related Agencies Appropriations Act, 2006.

Since the program's inception, the SBA has awarded WBCs a grant of up to $150,000 per year. Initially, the grant was awarded for one year, with the possibility of being renewed twice, for a total of up to three years. As a condition of the receipt of funds, the WBC was required to raise at least one non-federal dollar for each two federal dollars during the grant's first year (1:2), one non-federal dollar for each federal dollar during year two (1:1), and two non-federal dollars for each federal dollar during year three (2:1).

P.L. 105-135, the Small Business Reauthorization Act of 1997, authorized the SBA to award grants to WBCs for up to five years—one base year and four option years, subject to availability of funds and the recipient organization's compliance with federal law, SBA regulations, and terms and conditions specified in a cooperative agreement. In addition, the matching requirement was reduced to one non-federal dollar for each two federal dollars in years one through three rather than just during the first year (1:2), one non-federal dollar for each federal dollar in year four rather than during year two (1:1), and two non-federal dollars for each federal dollar in year five rather than in year three (2:1). In addition, not more than one-half of the non-federal matching assistance could be in the form of an in-kind contribution, including office equipment and office space.[35] The SBA was also required to "develop and implement an annual programmatic and financial examination of each" WBC.[36]

P.L. 106-17, the Women's Business Center Amendments Act of 1999, reduced the program's matching requirement to one non-federal dollar for each two federal dollars in years one and two (1:2), and one non-federal dollar for each federal dollar in years three, four and five (1:1).

P.L. 106-165, the Women's Business Centers Sustainability Act of 1999, authorized the SBA to create a WBC Sustainability Pilot Grant program. Subject to annual reauthorization, it provided WBCs that had completed the initial five year grant an opportunity to apply for an additional five year grant. Thus, the act allowed successful WBCs to receive SBA funding for a total of 10 years.

P.L. 110-28, the U.S. Troop Readiness, Veterans' Care, Katrina Recovery, and Iraq Accountability Appropriations Act, 2007, changed the federal share to not more than 50% for all grant years (1:1). It also allowed WBCs that successfully completed the initial five-year grant period to apply for an unlimited number of three-year funding renewals.

Today, there are 110 WBCs located throughout most of the United States and the territories.[37] In FY2010, they assisted 160,735 small business owners.[38] They also assisted in the formation of 689 new businesses in FY2010.[39] The WBC program's FY2010 funding was $23.5 million.[40]

As part of its legislative mandate to implement an annual programmatic and financial examination of each WBC, the SBA's Office of Entrepreneurial Development includes WBCs in its previously mentioned multi-year time series study of its programs.[41] The survey has been administered annually by a private firm. The latest survey findings were released on September 13, 2010.

The firm administering the 2009 survey of SBA management and training clients received 478 completed surveys from WBC clients.[42] The survey indicated that

- approximately 76% of WBC respondents reported that the information they received from their counselor was valuable,
- 78% of WBC respondents that received more than three hours of counseling rated WBC usefulness "high" as compared to 74% of respondents that received less than three hours of counseling, and
- 40% of start-up clients and 43% of in-business clients reported that they were able to increase sales as a result of WBC assistance.[43]

Microloan Technical Assistance Program

Congress authorized the SBA's Microloan lending program in 1991 (P.L. 102-140, the Departments of Commerce, Justice, and State, the Judiciary, and Related Agencies Appropriations Act, 1992) to address the perceived disadvantages faced by women, low-income, and minority entrepreneurs and business owners gaining access to capital for starting or expanding their business. The program became operational in 1992. Its stated purpose is

to assist women, low-income, veteran ... and minority entrepreneurs and business owners and other individuals possessing the capability to operate successful business concerns; to assist small business concerns in those areas suffering from a lack of credit due to economic downturns; ... to make loans to eligible intermediaries to enable such intermediaries to provide small-scale loans, particularly loans in amounts averaging not more than $10,000, to start-up, newly established, or growing small business concerns for working capital or the acquisition of materials, supplies, or equipment; [and] to make grants to eligible intermediaries that, together with non-Federal matching funds, will enable such intermediaries to provide intensive marketing, management, and technical assistance to microloan borrowers.[44]

Initially, the SBA's Microloan program was authorized as a five-year demonstration project. It was made permanent, subject to reauthorization, by P.L. 105-135, the Small Business Reauthorization Act of 1997.

The SBA's Microloan Technical Assistance Program, which is part of the SBA's Microloan program but receives a separate appropriation, provides grants to Microloan intermediaries to provide management and technical training assistance to Microloan program borrowers and prospective borrowers.[45] There are 162 intermediaries participating in the Microloan program.

Intermediaries are eligible to receive a Microloan technical assistance grant "of not more than 25% of the total outstanding balance of loans made to it" under the Microloan program.[46] Grant funds may be used only to provide marketing, management, and technical assistance to Microloan borrowers, except that up to 25% of the funds may be used to provide such assistance to prospective Microloan borrowers. Grant funds may also be used to attend training required by the SBA.[47]

In most instances, intermediaries must contribute, solely from non-federal sources, an amount equal to 25% of the grant amount.[48] In addition to cash or other direct funding, the contribution may include indirect costs or in-kind contributions paid for under non-federal programs.[49] Intermediaries which make at least 50% of their loans to small businesses located in or owned by residents of an Economically Distressed Area are not subject to the 25% contribution requirement.[50] Intermediaries may expend no more than 25% of the grant funds on third-party contracts for the provision of management and technical assistance.[51]

The SBA does not require Microloan borrowers to participate in the Microloan Technical Assistance Program. However, intermediaries typically require Microloan borrowers to participate in the training program as a condition of the receipt of a microloan. Combining loan and intensive management and technical assistance training is one of the Microloan program's distinguishing features.[52]

The Microloan Technical Assistance Program assisted 3,729 small business owners in FY2010.[53] Its FY2010 funding was $22.5 million.[54]

SCORE (Service Corps of Retired Executives)

The SBA has partnered with various voluntary business and professional service organizations to provide management and technical assistance training to small businesses since the 1950s. On October 5, 1964, then-SBA Administrator Eugene P. Foley officially launched SCORE (Service Corps of Retired Executives) as a national, volunteer organization with 2,000 members, uniting over 50 independent nonprofit organizations into a single, national nonprofit organization.[55] Since then, the SBA has provided financial assistance to SCORE to provide training to small business owners and prospective owners.[56]

Over the years, Congress has authorized the SBA to take certain actions relating to SCORE. For example, P.L. 89-754, the Demonstration Cities and Metropolitan Development Act of 1966, authorized the SBA to permit members of SCORE and other nonprofit organizations use of the SBA's office facilities and services. P.L. 90-104, the Small Business Act Amendments of 1967, added the authority to pay travel and subsistence expenses "incurred at the request of the Administration in connection with travel to a point more than fifty miles distant from the home of that individual in providing gratuitous services to small businessmen" or "in connection with attendance at meetings sponsored by the Administration."[57] P.L. 106-554, the Consolidated Appropriations Act, 2001 (Section 1(a)(9)—the Small Business Reauthorization Act of 2000) authorized SCORE to solicit cash and in-kind contributions from the private sector to be used to carry out its functions.

The SBA currently provides grants to SCORE to provide "in-person mentoring" and "nearly 7,000 local training workshops annually" to small businesses.[58] SCORE's 364 chapters and more than 800 branch offices are located throughout the United States and partner with nearly 13,000 volunteer counselors, who are working or retired business owners, executives and corporate leaders, to provide management and training assistance to small businesses.[59]

SCORE assisted 407,240 small business owners and prospective entrepreneurs in FY2010.[60] In FY2010, 1,077 new businesses were formed with assistance from SCORE counselors.[61] Its FY2010 funding was $11.1 million.[62]

W. Kenneth Yancey, Jr., SCORE's chief executive officer, provided the following description at a congressional hearing of SCORE's efforts to assist small businesses as they deal with the nation's current economic environment:

SCORE volunteers know things that only experience can teach. All across the country, SCORE is helping clients navigate the credit crunch. SCORE can mentor an aspiring entrepreneur through the business plan process to get them through the start-up phase. For in-business clients, SCORE can provide advice on handling cash flow problems and marketing to drive leads and sales. Many SCORE chapters offer team counseling, where a group of volunteers examine various aspects of the client's business and make recommendations.[63]

The SBA Office of Entrepreneurial Development includes SCORE in its multi-year time series study to assess its programs' effectiveness. The firm administering the 2009 survey of SBA management and training clients received 3,695 completed surveys from SCORE clients.[64] The survey indicated that

- approximately 74% of SCORE respondents reported that the information they received from their counselor was valuable,
- 77% of SCORE respondents that received three or more hours of counseling rated SCORE usefulness as "high" compared to 71% of respondents that received less than three hours of counseling, and
- 30% of start-up clients and 38% of in-business clients reported that they were able to increase sales as a result of SCORE assistance.[65]

Program for Investment in Micro-entrepreneurs

P.L. 106-102, the Gramm-Leach-Bliley Act (of 1999) (Subtitle C—Microenterprise Technical Assistance and Capacity Building Program) amended P.L. 103-325, the Riegle Community Development and Regulatory Improvement Act of 1994, to authorize the SBA to "establish a microenterprise technical assistance and capacity building grant program."[66] The program was to "provide assistance from the Administration in the form of grants" to

nonprofit microenterprise development organizations or programs (or a group or collaborative thereof) that has a demonstrated record of delivering microenterprise services to disadvantaged entrepreneurs; an intermediary; a microenterprise development organization or program that is accountable to a local community, working in conjunction with a state or local government or Indian tribe; or an Indian tribe acting on its own, if the Indian tribe can certify that no private organization or program referred to in this paragraph exists within its jurisdiction."[67]

The SBA was directed "to ensure that not less than 50% of the grants ... are used to benefit very low-income persons, including those residing on Indian reservations."[68] It was also directed to

(1) provide training and technical assistance to disadvantaged entrepreneurs; (2) provide training and capacity building services to microenterprise development organizations and programs and groups of such organizations to assist such organizations and programs in developing microenterprise training and services; (3) aid in researching and developing the best practices in the field of microenterprise and technical assistance programs for disadvantaged entrepreneurs; and (4) for such other activities as the Administrator determines are consistent with the purposes of this subtitle.[69]

The SBA's Program for Investment in Micro-entrepreneurs (PRIME) was designed to meet these legislative requirements by providing "assistance to organizations that help low-income entrepreneurs who lack sufficient training and education to gain access to capital to establish and expand their small businesses."[70] The program offers four types of grants:

- Technical Assistance Grants support training and technical assistance to disadvantaged micro-entrepreneurs,
- Capacity Building Grants support training and capacity building services to micro-enterprise development organizations and programs to assist them in developing micro-enterprise training and services,
- Research and Development Grants support the development and sharing of best practices in the field of micro-enterprise development and technical assistance programs for disadvantaged micro-entrepreneurs, and
- Discretionary Grants support other activities determined to be consistent with these purposes.[71]

Grants are awarded on an annual basis. Applicants may be approved for option year funding for up to four subsequent years. Award amounts vary depending on the availability of funds. However, no single grantee may receive more than $250,000 or 10% of the total funds made available for the program in a single fiscal year, whichever is less.[72]

Recipients must match 50% of the funding from non-federal sources. Revenue from fees, grants, and gifts; income from loan sources; and in-kind resources from non-federal public or private sources may be used to comply with the matching requirement.[73] SBA regulations indicate that "applicants or grantees with severe constraints on available sources of matching funds may request that the Administrator or designee reduce or eliminate the matching requirements."[74] Any reductions or eliminations must not exceed 10% of the aggregate of all PRIME grant funds made available by SBA in any fiscal year.[75]

The SBA awarded 92 PRIME grants to management and technical assistance service providers in FY2010, ranging from $50,000 to $250,000.[76] The number of clients served by this program during FY2010 is unavailable. The PRIME program's funding in FY2010 was $8.1 million.[77]

Veterans Business Development Programs

The SBA has supported management and technical assistance training for veteran-owned small businesses since its formation as an agency. However, during the 1990s, some in Congress noted that a direct loan program for veterans was eliminated by the SBA in 1995 and that the "training and counseling for veterans dropped from 38,775 total counseling sessions for veterans in 1993 to 29,821 sessions in 1998."[78] Concerned that "the needs of veterans have been diminished systematically at the SBA," Congress adopted P.L. 106-50, the Veterans Entrepreneurship and Small Business Development Act of 1999.[79] It authorized the establishment of the federally chartered National Veterans Business Development Corporation (now also known as The Veterans Corporation) to

> (1) expand the provision of and improve access to technical assistance regarding entrepreneurship for the Nation's veterans; and (2) to assist veterans, including service-disabled veterans, with the formation and expansion of small business concerns by working with and organizing public and private resources, including those of the Small Business Administration, the Department of Veterans Affairs, the Department of Labor, the Department of Commerce, the Department of Defense, the Service Corps of Retired Executives ..., the Small Business Development Centers ..., and the business development staffs of each department and agency of the United States.[80]

The act re-emphasized the SBA's responsibility "to reach out to and include veterans in its programs providing financial and technical assistance."[81] It also included veterans as a target group for the SBA's 7(a), 504/CDC, and Microloan programs. It also required the SBA to enter into a memorandum of understanding with SCORE to, among other things, establish "a program to coordinate counseling and training regarding entrepreneurship to veterans through the chapters of SCORE throughout the United States."[82] It also directed the SBA to enter into a memorandum of understanding with small business development centers, the Department of Veteran Affairs, and the National Veterans Business Development Corporation "with respect to entrepreneurial assistance to veterans, including service-disabled veterans."[83] The act specified that the following services were to be provided:

(1) Conducting of studies and research, and the distribution of information generated by such studies and research, on the formation, management, financing, marketing, and operation of small business concerns by veterans.
(2) Provision of training and counseling to veterans concerning the formation, management, financing, marketing, and operation of small business concerns.
(3) Provision of management and technical assistance to the owners and operators of small business concerns regarding international markets, the promotion of exports, and the transfer of technology.
(4) Provision of assistance and information to veterans regarding procurement opportunities with Federal, State, and local agencies, especially such agencies funded in whole or in part with Federal funds.
 (5) Establishment of an information clearinghouse to collect and distribute information, including by electronic means, on the assistance programs of Federal, State, and local governments, and of the private sector, including information on office locations, key personnel, telephone numbers, mail and electronic addresses, and contracting and subcontracting opportunities.
(6) Provision of Internet or other distance learning academic instruction for veterans in business subjects, including accounting, marketing, and business fundamentals.
(7) Compilation of a list of small business concerns owned and controlled by service-disabled veterans that provide products or services that could be procured by the United States and delivery of such list to each department and agency of the United States. Such list shall be delivered in hard copy and electronic form and shall include

the name and address of each such small business concern and the products or services that it provides.[84]

The SBA's Office of Veterans Business Development (OVBD) was established to address these statutory requirements by promoting "veterans' small business ownership by conducting comprehensive outreach, through program and policy development and implementation, ombudsman support, coordinated Agency initiatives, and direct assistance to veterans, service-disabled veterans, Reserve and National Guard members, and discharging active duty personnel."[85]

The OVBD provided, or supported third-parties to provide, management and technical assistance training services to 122,901 veterans during FY2009. These services were provided "through SBA district offices; OVBD-developed and distributed materials; websites; partnering; management of regional Veterans Business Outreach Centers; direct guidance and assistance to Agency veteran customers; inter-agency assistance with federal partners; and through enhancements to intra-agency programs used by the military and veteran communities."[86] For example, OVBD provided "207 public presentations and training events to enhance veterans' understanding of and access to SBA programs and partners to improve access to broader federal procurement opportunities, initiatives, and programs for veterans and for service-disabled veterans."[87] It also regularly referred veterans to SBA district offices and SBA management and technical assistance training resource partners for locally based training, workshops and assistance.[88] The OVBD's FY2010 funding was $7.6 million.[89]

The OVBD's Veterans Business Outreach Centers Program is one of its larger and better known third-party provider management and technical assistance training programs. It was established by the SBA under the authority in section 8(b)(17) of the Small Business Act. It is to "provide outreach, assessment, long term counseling, training, coordinated service delivery referrals, mentoring & network building, procurement assistance and E-based assistance to benefit Small Business concerns and potential concerns owned and controlled by Veterans, Service Disabled Veterans and Members of Reserve Components of the U.S. Military."[90]

There are currently 16 Veterans Business Outreach Centers. Each center is funded on an annual basis, with funding not to exceed $150,000 each year. Awards "may vary, depending upon location, staff size, project objectives, performance and agency priorities, and additional special nitiatives initiated by the Office of Veterans Business Development."[91] Existing centers may receive additional funding for special outreach or other initiatives. The initial grant award is for 12 months, with the possibility of four additional (option) years.

In FY2009, the Veterans Business Outreach Centers Program conducted its fifth annual "Customer Satisfaction Survey." The centers surveyed 2% of their total veteran customer population. The FY2009 survey found that

> 89.3% of the clients using the centers were satisfied or highly satisfied with the quality, relevance and timeliness of the assistance provided. Clients evaluating the centers gave 89.3% ratings for the training programs provided and 89.3% ratings for program evaluation.[92]

7(j) Management and Technical Assistance Program

Utilizing what it viewed as broad statutory powers granted under Section 8(a) of the Small Business Act of 1958, as amended, the SBA issued regulations in 1970 creating the 8(a) contracting program to "assist small concerns owned by disadvantaged persons to become self-sufficient, viable businesses capable of competing effectively in the market place."[93] Utilizing its statutory authority under Section 7(j) of the Small Business Act to provide management and technical assistance through contracts, grants and cooperative agreement to qualified service providers, the regulations specified that "the SBA may provide technical and management assistance to assist in the performance of the subcontracts."[94]

On October 24, 1978, P.L. 95-507, to amend the Small Business Act and the Small Business Investment Act of 1958, provided the SBA explicit statutory authority to extend financial, management, technical, and other services to socially and economically disadvantaged small businesses. The SBA's current regulations indicate that the 7(j) Management and Technical Assistance Program, named after the section of the Small Business Act of 1958, as amended, authorizing the SBA to provide management and technical assistance training, will, "through its private sector service providers" deliver "a wide variety of management and technical assistance to eligible individuals or concerns to meet their specific needs, including: (a) counseling and training in the areas of financing, management, accounting, bookkeeping, marketing, and operation of small business concerns; and (b) the identification and development of new business opportunities."[95] Eligible individuals and businesses include "8(a) certified firms, small disadvantaged businesses,

businesses operating in areas of high unemployment, or low income or firms owned by low income individuals."[96]

In FY2010, the 7(j) Management and Technical Assistance Program awarded four training contracts totaling $1.5 million, ranging from $310,000 to $455,000; one grant for International Trade technical assistance for $250,000, and one interagency Agreement for $150,000 to the Department of Commerce's Minority Business Development Agency. The 7(j) program assisted 3,480 small business owners in FY2010.[97] Its FY2010 funding was $6.58 million.[98]

Native American Outreach Program

The SBA established the Office of Native American Affairs in 1994 to "address the unique needs of America's First people."[99] It oversees the Native American Outreach Program, which provides management and technical educational assistance to American Indians, Alaska Natives, Native Hawaiians and "the indigenous people of Guam and American Samoa ... to promote entity-owned and individual 8(a) certification, government contracting, entrepreneurial education, and capital access."[100] The program's management and technical assistance services are available to members of these groups living in most areas of the nation.[101] However, "for Native Americans living in much of Indian Country, actual reservations communities where the land is held in trust by the U.S. federal government, SBA loan guaranties and technical assistance services are not available."[102]

The SBA's Office of Native American Affairs has four goals:

- to increase financial literacy across a broad section of the community and to educate internally on the roles of tribal governments;
- to formulate an SBA-specific tribal consultation policy to engage with tribally run economic development branches;
- to conduct a Native American veterans' outreach initiative to increase the utilization of the SBA's counseling services and the Patriot Express loan guaranty program; and
- to conduct an in-depth market research analysis to fine tune marketing efforts ending in a comprehensive communications plan to reach the target market with the end goal being a measurable increase in the use of all SBA tools with particular emphasis on loans and contracting.[103]

Data concerning the number of clients served by the Native American Outreach Program for FY2010 is not available. From May 2009 through the end of FY2009, the program served 1,221 clients.[104] The Native American Outreach program's FY2010 funding was $4.05 million.[105]

DEPARTMENT OF COMMERCE SMALL BUSINESS MANAGEMENT AND TECHNICAL ASSISTANCE TRAINING PROGRAMS

As mentioned previously, the Department of Commerce's Minority Business Development Agency provides training to minority business owners to assist them in becoming suppliers to private corporations and the federal government.[106] In addition, the Department of Commerce's Economic Development Administration's Local Technical Assistance Program promotes efforts to build and expand local organizational capacity in distressed areas. As part of that effort, it funds projects that focus on technical or market feasibility studies of economic development projects or programs, which often include consultation with small businesses.[107]

The Minority Business Development Agency

The Minority Business Development Agency (MBDA) was established by President Richard M. Nixon by Executive Order 11625, issued on October 13, 1971, and published in the *Federal Register* the next day. It clarified the authority of the Secretary of Commerce to:

- implement federal policy in support of the minority business enterprise program,
- provide additional technical and management assistance to disadvantaged businesses,
- assist in demonstration projects, and
- coordinate the participation of all federal departments and agencies in an increased minority enterprise effort.[108]

The MBDA's FY2010 appropriation was $31.5 million.

As part of its mission, the MBDA seeks to train minority business owners to become first- or second-tier suppliers to private corporations and the federal government. Progress is measured in the business's increased gross receipts, number of employees, and size and scale of the firms associated with minority business enterprises.

According to the MBDA's annual report:

> In fiscal year 2008 the Return on Agency Investment (ROAI) was $74. The ROAI is one of several indicators that the agency uses to track overall performance. This measure takes all agency appropriations ($28.6 million) and divides it by the total dollars of obtained closed transactions for financials and contracts. Accomplishments were reported by a total of 44 funded projects that were funded across the country. These projects, along with agency staff, reported that they were successful in securing over $1 billion dollars in contracts and over $1 billion dollars in closed financial transactions.
>
> MBDA funded two flagship programs, the (Minority and Native American) Business Enterprise Centers (BECs) and the Minority Business Opportunity Centers (MBOCs). The BEC program services minority business entrepreneurs through the Minority Business Enterprise Centers (MBECs) and through the Native American Business Enterprise Centers (NABECs). Technically, the BECs are the primary drivers of the agency. It is through this program that the majority of MBDA's success is accomplished.
>
> The 36 BEC projects which were funded in FY 2008 secured close to $700 million in contracts and over $1 billion in closed financial transactions for their minority clients. By comparison, the BEC program reported accomplishments of $619.5 million in contracts and $398.3 million in secured financial transactions in FY2007.[109]

The EDA Local Technical Assistance Program

P.L. 89-186, the Public Works and Economic Development Act of 1965, authorized the Department of Commerce's Economic Development Administration (EDA) to provide financial assistance to economically distressed areas in the United States that are characterized by high levels of unemployment and low per-capita income. The EDA currently administers seven Economic Development Assistance Programs (EDAPs) that award matching grants for public works, economic adjustment, planning, technical assistance, research and evaluation, trade adjustment assistance, and global climate change mitigation.[110] In FY2010, these programs were appropriated $293 million.

Grants awarded under the EDA's Local Technical Assistance Program are designed to help solve specific economic development problems, respond to development opportunities, and build and expand local organizational capacity in distressed areas.[111] The majority of local technical assistance projects focus on technical or market feasibility studies of economic development projects or programs, including consultation with small businesses. In FY2010, technical assistance accounted for 3.8% of the total economic development program allocation for the EDA, or $9.8 million.

CONGRESSIONAL ISSUES

For many years, a recurring theme at congressional hearings concerning the SBA's management and technical assistance training programs has been the perceived need to improve program efficiency by eliminating duplication of services and increasing cooperation and coordination both within and among SCORE, WBCs, and SBDCs.[112] As mentioned previously, on March 15, 2011, the House Committee on Small Business recommended to the House Committee on the Budget that several SBA management and technical assistance training programs be defunded "because they duplicate existing programs at the SBA or at other agencies."[113] The committee recommended that funding for Women Development Centers, Veterans Business Outreach Centers, the Program for Investment in Micro-entrepreneurs (PRIME), HUBZone outreach, the Office of Native American Affairs, Regional Innovation Centers, the State Trade and Export Promotion Pilot Program, the Drug-Free Workplace Program, and the Emerging Leaders Program be ended.[114]

In recent years, Congress has also explored ways to improve the SBA's measurement of the programs' effectiveness. Congress has also paid increased attention to the impact of national economic conditions on WBC and SBDC finances and their capacity to meet federal matching requirements and to maintain client service levels.[115]

Program Administration

In 2007, the U.S. Government Accountability Office (GAO) was asked to assess the SBA's oversight of WBCs and the coordination and duplication of services among the SBA's management and technical training assistance programs. GAO found that

> As described in the terms of the SBA award, WBCs are required to coordinate with local SBDCs and SCORE chapters. In addition, SBA officials told us that they expected district offices to ensure that the programs did not duplicate each other. However, based on our review, WBCs lacked guidance and information from SBA on how to successfully carry out their coordination efforts. Most of the WBCs that we spoke with explained that in some situations they referred clients to an SBDC or SCORE counselor, and some WBCs also took steps to more actively coordinate with local SBDCs and SCORE chapters to avoid duplication and leverage resources. We learned that WBCs used a variety of approaches to facilitate coordination, such as memorandums of understanding, information-sharing meetings, and co-locating staff and services. However, some WBCs told us that they faced challenges in coordinating services with SBDC and SCORE, in part because the programs have similar performance measures, and this could result in competition among the service providers in some locations. We also found that on some occasions SBA encouraged WBCs to provide services that were similar to services already provided by SBDCs in their district. Such challenges thwart coordination efforts and could increase the risk of duplication in some geographic areas.[116]

Some organizations have argued that the SBA's management and technical assistance training programs should be merged. For example, the U.S. Women's Chamber of Commerce has argued that

> over the last 50 years, the SBA entrepreneurial development system has grown into a fragmented array of programs, which has resulted in a disorganized, overlapping, and [in]efficient delivery of service through a system that is ill-prepared to effectively address the challenges of our economy....
> if we are to serve the needs of American entrepreneurs, we must commit to a top to bottom restructuring of the delivery of the entrepreneurial services of the SBA. The myriad of entrepreneurial

development programs should be unified into one centrally managed organization that has the flexibility to provide services when and where they are needed.[117]

These organizations argue that merging the SBA's management and technical assistance training programs would provide greater coordination of services and "one clear channel for assistance" that "is paramount to the average business owner seeking help."[118] Advocates of merging the SBA's management and technical assistance training programs often mention merging them into the SBDC Program because, in their view, it has the advantage of having a broader connection to mainstream resources and its locations are "greater and more diverse" than other SBA management and technical assistance training programs.[119]

Others argue that providing separate management and training assistance programs for specific groups is the best means to ensure that those group's unique challenges are recognized and their unique needs are met.[120] For example, when asked at a congressional hearing about the rationale for having separate management and technical assistance training programs for specific groups, a representative of the Association of Women's Business Centers stated:

> I think that there is tremendous rationale for having different programs.... The women's business center programs really target a very different kind of population than the SBDCs.... We serve very different clientele.... We create a very different culture at the women's business center. We really have made it a welcoming place where ... they feel comfortable.... And it's very important to me that the woman have a place where they feel comfortable ... and where they see other women like themselves who are aspiring to reach their dreams.[121]

At another congressional hearing, the Association of Women's Business Centers' Executive Director argued that "the new three-year funding arrangement" for WBCs had enabled them to "concentrate on better serving their clients and growing their programs" and that WBCs should be provided continued and expanded funding because they provide effective services:

> We know that when our program performance is measured against any other enterprise assistance program, we will meet or exceed any performance measures. Indeed, the SBA's own client-based

performance reviews have shown our clients to be just as satisfied or in some cases more satisfied with the services they have received compared to the SBA's other entrepreneurial development efforts.[122]

Instead of merging programs, some argue that improved communication among the SBA's management and technical assistance training resource partners and enhanced SBA program oversight is needed. For example, during the 111th Congress, the House passed H.R. 2352, the Job Creation Through Entrepreneurship Act of 2009, on May 20, 2009, by a vote of 406–15. The Senate did not take action on the bill. In its committee report accompanying the bill, the House Committee on Small Business concluded that

> Each ED [Entrepreneurial Development] program has a unique mandate and service delivery approach that is customized to its particular clients. However, as a network, the programs have established local connections and resources that benefit entrepreneurs within a region. Enhanced coordination among this network is critical to make the most of scarce resources available for small firms. It can also ensure that best practices are shared amongst providers that have similar goals but work within different contexts.[123]

In an effort to enhance the oversight and coordination of the SBA's management and technical assistance training programs, the Job Creation Through Entrepreneurship Act of 2009 would have

- required the SBA to create a new online, multilingual distance training and education program that was fully integrated into the SBA's existing management and technical assistance training programs and "allows entrepreneurs and small business owners the opportunity to exchange technical assistance through the sharing of information."[124]
- required the SBA to coordinate its management and technical assistance training programs "with State and local economic development agencies and other federal agencies as appropriate."[125]
- required the SBA to "report annually to Congress, in consultation with other federal departments and agencies as appropriate, on opportunities to foster coordination, limit duplication, and improve program delivery for federal entrepreneurial development activities."[126]

Program Evaluation

GAO noted in its 2007 assessment of the SBA's management and technical assistance training programs that, in addition to its annual survey of WBC, SBDC, and SCORE participants, the SBA requires WBCs to provide quarterly performance reports that include "the WBCs' actual accomplishments, compared with their performance goals for the reporting period; actual budget expenditures, compared with an estimated budget; cost of client fees; success stories; and names of WBC personnel and board members."[127] GAO also noted that WBCs are also required to issue fourth quarter performance reports that "also include a summary of the year's activities and economic impact data that the WBCs collect from their clients, such as number of business startups, number of jobs created, and gross receipts."[128] SBDCs have similar reporting requirements.[129]

In recent years, Congress has considered requiring the SBA to expand its use of outcome-based measures to determine the effectiveness of its management and technical training assistance programs. For example, the previously mentioned Job Creation Through Entrepreneurship Act of 2009 would have required the SBA to create "outcome-based measures of the amount of job creation or economic activity generated in the local community as a result of efforts made and services provided by each women's business center."[130] It would also would have required the SBA to "develop and implement a consistent data collection process to cover all entrepreneurial development programs" including "data relating to job creation, performance, and any other data determined appropriate by the Administrator with respect to the Administration's entrepreneurial development programs."[131]

WBC and SBDC Finances

In recent years, Congress has provided increased attention to the impact of national economic conditions on WBC and SBDC finances and their capacity to meet federal matching requirements and to maintain client service levels.[132] For example, Donald Wilson, president, Association of Small Business Development Centers, testified before Congress that national economic conditions were making it more difficult for SBDCs to raise the funds necessary to meet federal matching requirements:

One of the issues is the whole design of the program [where] the federal dollar would leverage the non-federal dollar. And so when you get states that match and the federal dollar never goes up, the states are not likely to go up.

And now with this current economic downturn, all you have to do is look at foundations and you see where their stock portfolios are going. You see banks which have often been very helpful for us because we bring them high quality loan candidates. Their dollars are declining. States that are facing severe budget deficits which by law by their state constitution they cannot have. They are cutting back.

And so the issue now is not the same rosy outlook in terms of getting matched that it was, say, three or four years ago, and quite frankly, we encounter all the time if the federal government does not believe in this program, you know, we are not going to start pouring a lot of money into it.[133]

P.L. 111-240, the Small Business Jobs Act of 2010, authorizes changes to several SBA programs, including the SBA's management and training programs.[134] For example, as mentioned previously, the act authorizes $50 million in additional funds for SBDCs to provide targeted technical assistance to small businesses for various specified activities, such as seeking access to capital or credit, federal procurement opportunities, and opportunities to export products. It also authorizes the SBA to temporarily waive, in whole or in part, for successive fiscal years, the nonfederal share matching requirement relating to "technical assistance and counseling" for WBCs under the following specified circumstances: the economic conditions affecting the center, the waiver's impact on the WBC program's credibility, the WBC's demonstrated ability to raise nonfederal funds, and the WBC's performance.[135] The non-federal share requirement can not be waived in FY2013, or any fiscal year thereafter.[136]

In addition, S. 3967, the Small Business Investment and Innovation Act of 2010, which was introduced on November 18, 2010, would authorize changes to several SBA programs, including the SBA's training and technical assistance programs.[137] For example, the bill would

- increase SCORE's funding to $13 million in FY2011, $15 million in FY2012, and $18 million in FY2013.
- increase WBC funding to $20 million in FY2011, $20.5 million in FY2012, and $21 million in FY2013.

- require the SBA Administrator to "maximize the transparency of the WBC financial assistance proposal process and the WBC programmatic and financial oversight process" by (1) providing public notice of announcements for financial assistance and grants not later than the end of the first quarter of each fiscal year, (2) providing in the announcements an outline of the award and program evaluation criteria used, including a description of the weighting of the criteria used, (3) minimizing paperwork and reporting requirements for applicants for and recipients of financial assistance, (4) standardizing the WBC program's oversight and review process, and (5) providing to each WBC, "not later than 60 days after the completion of a site visit (whether conducted for an audit, performance review, or other reason), a copy of site visit reports and evaluation reports prepared by district office technical representatives or officers or employees of the Administration."[138]

- direct the Comptroller General to study the unique economic issues facing WBCs located in predominately rural, urban, and insular areas, including the difficulties these centers face (1) raising non-federal funds, (2) competing for financial assistance, non-federal funds, or other types of assistance, (3) writing grant proposals, and (4) any other difficulty which may result from the economic circumstances of the area in which they are located. The Comptroller General would be required to submit to Congress a report regarding the results of the study within one year of the bill's enactment.

- increase Veteran Business Centers' funding to $8 million in FY2011, $8.5 million in FY2012, and $9 million in FY2013.

- establish an Associate Administrator of the Office of Native American Affairs to implement training and technical assistance programs for the development of business enterprises by Native Americans and to establish Native American business centers which would be awarded funding for five-year projects that offer culturally tailored business development assistance to Native Americans.

- authorize $10 million in FY2011, $10 million in FY2012, and $10 million in FY2013 for the Native American business center program.

CONCLUDING OBSERVATIONS

Congressional interest in the federal government's small business management and technical assistance training programs has increased in recent years. One of the reasons for the heightened level of interest in these programs is that small business has led job formation and retention during previous economic recoveries.[139] It has been argued that effective small business management and technical assistance training programs are needed if small businesses are to lead job creation and retention during the current economic recovery. As Representative Heath Shuler stated during a congressional hearing,

> We often talk about the role that small business plays in the creation of jobs and with good reason. Small firms generate between 60 and 80 percent of new positions. Following the recession in the mid-1990s, they created 3.8 million jobs.... we could use that growth today. But unfortunately, many firms are struggling to make ends meet. Let's allow them to hire new workers. In the face of historic economic challenges, we should be investing in America's job creators. SBA's Entrepreneurial Development Programs, or ED, do just that. Of all the tools in the small business toolbox, these are some of the most critical. They help small firms do everything from draft business plans to access capital.[140]

There is a general consensus that federal management and technical assistance training programs serve an important purpose and, for the most part, are providing needed services that are not available elsewhere. As Karen Mills, SBA Administrator, stated during a press interview:

> We find that our counseling operations are equally important as our credit operations because small businesses really need help and advice, and when they get it, they tend to have more sales and more profits and more longevity, and they hire more people. So we have looked forward and said, "How do we get all the tools small businesses need into their hands?" Maybe they want to export. Maybe they want to know how to use broadband. Maybe they are veterans who are coming back and want to start a business or grow their business. Our job is to make sure all that information and opportunity is accessible for small businesses so they can do what they do, which is keep our economy strong.[141]

There is also a general consensus that making federal management and technical assistance training programs more effective and responsive to the needs of small business would assist the national economic recovery. However, there are disagreements over how to achieve that goal.

Some advocate increasing funding for existing programs to enable them to provide additional training opportunities for small businesses while, at the same time, maintaining separate training programs for specific demographic groups as a means to ensure that those groups' specific needs are met; require the SBA to make more extensive use of outcome-based measures to better determine the programs' effect on small business formation and retention, job creation and retention, and the generation of wealth; and temporarily reduce or eliminate federal matching requirements to enable SBA's management and technical assistance training resource partners to focus greater attention to service delivery and less to fund raising. Others argue for a merger of existing programs to reduce costs and improve program efficiency, to focus available resources on augmenting the capacity of SBDCs to meet the needs of all small business groups, and require the SBA to make more extensive use of outcome-based performance measures to determine program effectiveness.

There are no case studies or empirical data available concerning the efficiencies that might be gained by merging the SBA's management and technical assistance training programs. Advocates argue that merging the programs would improve communications, reduce confusion by business owners seeking assistance by ensuring that all small business management and technical assistance training centers serve all small business owners and aspiring entrepreneurs, lead to more sustainable and predictable funding for the programs from non-federal sources, and result in more consistent and standard operating procedures throughout the country.[142] Opponents argue that any gains in program efficiency that might be realized would be more than offset by the loss of targeted services for constituencies that often require different information and training to meet their unique challenges and needs.[143]

APPENDIX.

Table A-1. Brief Descriptions of SBA Management and Technical Assistance Training Programs

Program Name	Authority	Brief Description	Number	Federal Matching Requirement
Small Business Development Center Grant Program	P.L. 96-302, 1980	Provides management and technical assistance training to small businesses through centers located in leading universities, colleges, and state economic development agencies.	About 1,000	50% match from non-federal sources comprised of not less than 50% cash and not more than 50% of indirect costs.
Women Business Center Grant Program	P.L. 100-533, 1988	Provides long-term training, counseling, networking, and mentoring to women entrepreneurs, especially those who are socially and economically disadvantaged.	110	50% match from non-federal sources; not more than one-half of the non-federal matching assistance may be in the form of in-kind contributions, including office equipment and office space.
SCORE ((Service Corps of Retired Executives)	Section 8(b) of the Small Business Act; P.L. 89-754, 1966	Provides technical, managerial, and informational assistance to small business concerns through in-person	364 chapters and 800+ branch offices	none

Table A-1. (Continued)

Program Name	Authority	Brief Description	Number	Federal Matching Requirement
		mentoring by volunteer counselors who are working or, in most instances, retired business owners.		
7(j) Technical Assistance Program	Section 7(j) of the Small Business Act; Section 8(a) of the Small Business Act; P.L. 95-507, 1978	Provides technical assistance training to 8(a) certified firms, small disadvantaged businesses, businesses operating in areas of high unemployment or low-income and firms owned by low-income individuals.	5 service providers and 1 interagency agreement	none
Microloan Technical Assistance Program	P.L. 102-140, 1992	Provides management and technical assistance training to Microloan borrowers and, within specified limits, to prospective Microloan borrowers.	162 intermediaries	25% from non-federal sources; no matching requirement if the intermediary makes at least 50% of its loans in an Economically Distressed Area.
Native American Outreach Program	Section 7(j) of the Small Business Act; SBA regulations, 1994	Provides management and technical assistance training to American Indians, Alaska Natives, Native Hawaiians	NA	none

Program Name	Authority	Brief Description	Number	Federal Matching Requirement
		and "the indigenous people of Guam and American Samoa … to promote entity-owned and individual 8(a) certification, government contracting, entrepreneurial education, and capital access."		
PRIME Technical Assistance Program	P.L. 106-102, 1999	Provides assistance in the form of grants to nonprofit microenterprise development organizations or programs that has a demonstrated record of delivering microenterprise services to disadvantaged entrepreneurs.	92 service providers	50% from non-federal sources; sources such as fees, grants, gifts, income from loan sources, and in-kind resources from non-federal public or private sources may be used to comply with the matching funds requirement
Veterans Business Development Programs	P.L. 106-50, 1999	The mission of the SBA's Office of Veterans Business Development is to (1) expand the provision of and improve access to technical assistance regarding entrepreneurship for the Nation's veterans; and	NA	none

Table A-1. (Continued)

Program Name	Authority	Brief Description	Number	Federal Matching Requirement
		(2) to assist veterans, including service-disabled veterans, with the formation and expansion of small business concerns by working with and organizing public and private resources, including those of the SBA.		

Source: Federal statutes, cited in table.

End Notes

[1] U.S. Small Business Administration, "Fiscal Year 2011 Congressional Budget Justification and FY2009 Annual Performance Report," Washington, DC: GPO, 2010, p. 1.

[2] U.S. Congress, Senate Committee on Banking and Currency, *Extension of the Small Business Act of 1953*, report to accompany S. 2127, 84th Cong., 1st sess., July 22, 1955, S.Rept. 84-1350 (Washington: GPO, 1955), p. 17.

[3] U.S. Small Business Administration, *Agency Financial Report, Fiscal Year 2010* (Washington, DC: GPO, 2010), p. 7.

[4] U.S. Small Business Administration, "Fiscal Year 2011 Congressional Budget Justification and FY2009 Annual Performance Report," Washington, DC: GPO, 2010, p. 4; SCORE (Service Corps of Retired Executives), "About SCORE," Washington, DC, http://www.score.org/explore_score.html; and U.S. Small Business Administration, Office of Congressional and Legislative Affairs, correspondence with the author, January 19, 2011.

[5] U.S. Small Business Administration, "Fiscal Year 2011 Congressional Budget Justification and FY2009 Annual Performance Report," Washington, DC: GPO, 2010, p. 4.

[6] U.S. Department of Commerce, Minority Business Development Agency, *Annual Performance Report, Fiscal Year 2008*, Washington, DC, 2009, p. 6, http://www.mbda.gov/? section_id= 2&bucket_id=643&content_id=3205&well=entire_page&portal_document_download=true &download_cid=3205&name=MBDA_Annual_Performance_Report_2008.pdf&legacy_ flag=false.

[7] 13 C.F.R. § 306.

[8] Representative Sam Graves, "Opening Statement for Views and Estimates Markup," Washington, DC, March 15, 2011, http://www.smallbusiness.house.gov/Calendar/Event Single. aspx? EventID= 227626. Also, see U.S. Congress, House Committee on Small Business, "Views and Estimates of the Committee on Small Business on Matters to be set forth in the Concurrent Resolution on the Budget for FY2012, communication to the Chairman, House Committee on the Budget," 112th Cong., 1st sess., March 17, 2011, http://smbiz.house.gov/UploadedFiles/ March_17_Views_and_Estimates_Letter.pdf. The management and technical assistance training programs recommended to be defunded include Women Development Centers, Veterans Business Outreach Centers, Program for Investment in Micro-entrepreneurs (PRIME), HUBZone outreach, Office of Native American Affairs, Regional Innovation Centers, State Trade and Export Promotion Pilot Program, the Drug-Free Workplace Program, and the Emerging Leaders Program.

[9] U.S. Small Business Administration, "Regional Clusters Initiative," Washington, DC, http:// www. sba. gov/ content/ regional-cluster-initiative-0.

[10] Ibid.

[11] Ibid.

[12] Ibid.; and U.S. Small Business Administration, Press Office, "SBA Announces Funding Available to Support Regional Clusters, Job Creation," Washington, DC, June 22, 2010, http://www.sba.gov/about-sba-services/7367/5732.

[13] U.S. Small Business Administration, Press Office, "SBA Announces Support for 10 Regional 'Innovative Economies' Clusters, Local Job Creation," Washington, DC, September 20, 2010, http://www.sba.gov/about-sba-services/7367/5590.

[14] U.S. Small Business Administration, Press Office, "SBA Announces Funding Available to Support Regional Clusters, Job Creation," Washington, DC, June 22, 2010, p. 2, http://www.sba. gov/ about-sba-services/7367/5732.

[15] Association of Small Business Development Centers, "A Brief History of America's Small Business Development Center Network," Burke, VA, http://www.asbdc-us.org/About_Us/ aboutus_history.html.

[16] Ibid.; and U.S. Congress, Senate Committee on Small Business, *Oversight of the Small Business Administration's Small Business Development Center Program*, 98th Cong., 1st sess., February 8, 1983, S.Hrg. 98-31 (Washington: GPO, 1983), p. 2.

[17] U.S. Congress, Senate Committee on Small Business, *Oversight of the Small Business Administration's Small Business Development Center Program*, 98th Cong., 1st sess., February 8, 1983, S.Hrg. 98-31 (Washington: GPO, 1983), p. 2.

[18] Ibid., p. 4.

[19] 15 U.S.C. 648(a)(4)(C).

[20] Ibid.; and P.L. 106-554, the Consolidated Appropriations Act, 2001.

[21] For American Samoa, Guam, and the U.S. Virgin Islands, the SBA is required to waive the matching requirements on awards less than $200,000 and has discretion to waive the match for awards exceeding $200,000. See 48 U.S.C. Sec. 1469a. Also, there is one exception to the disallowance of federal funds as a cash match. Community Development Block Grant (CDBG) funds received from the Department of Housing and Urban Development are allowed when: (1) the SBDC activities are consistent with the authorized CDBG activities for which the funds were granted; and (2) the CDBG activities are identified in the Consolidated Plan of the CDBG grantee or in the agreement between the CDBG grantee and the subrecipient of the funds.

[22] U.S. Small Business Administration, "Small Business Development Center Fy/Cy 2011 Program Announcement for Renewal of the Cooperative Agreement for Current Recipient Organizations," Washington, DC, p. 3, http://archive.sba.gov/idc/groups/public/documents/ sba_program_office/sbdc_2011_prgm_announce.pdf.

[23] Ibid.

[24] Association of Small Business Development Centers, "Welcome," Burke, Virginia, http:// www. asbdc -us.org/; and U.S. Small Business Administration, "FY2011 Congressional Budget Justification and FY2009 Annual Performance Report," Washington, DC, 2010, p. 53.

[25] U.S. Small Business Administration, Office of Congressional and Legislative Affairs, correspondence with the author, January 14, 2011.

[26] U.S. Small Business Administration, Office of Congressional and Legislative Affairs, correspondence with the author, January 19, 2011.

[27] P.L. 111-240, the Small Business Jobs Act of 2010, Sec. 1402. Grants for SBDCs. In addition, not less than 80% of the funding shall be used for counseling of small business concerns and not more than 20% may be used for classes and seminars. Total funding for SBDCs was $130 million in FY2010.

[28] U.S. Small Business Administration, "FY2011 Congressional Budget Justification and FY2009 Annual Performance Report," Washington, DC, 2010, p. 53.

[29] U.S. Small Business Administration, *Agency Financial Report, Fiscal Year 2010* (Washington, DC: GPO, 2010), p. 11.

[30] U.S. Small Business Administration, Office of Entrepreneurial Development, "Impact Study of Entrepreneurial Development Resources," Washington, DC, September 10, 2009, p. 2, http://archive.sba.gov/idc/groups/public/documents/sba_program_office/ed_finalreport_ 2009.pdf.

[31] U.S. Small Business Administration, Office of Entrepreneurial Development, "Impact Study of Entrepreneurial Development Resources," Washington, DC, September 13, 2010, p. 4, http://www.sba.gov/sites/default/files/09-10%20SBA%20ED%20Resources%20Impact%20 Study%20Final%20Report.pdf.

[32] Ibid., p. 8.

[33] Ibid., pp. 47-51.

[34] U.S. Congress, House Committee on Small Business, *Review of Women's Business Center Program*, 106th Cong., February 11, 1999, Serial No. 106-2 (Washington: GPO, 1999), p. 4.

[35] P.L. 105-135, the Small Business Reauthorization Act of 1997, Sec. 29. Women's Business Center Program.

[36] Ibid.

[37] U.S. Small Business Administration, Office of Congressional and Legislative Affairs, correspondence with the author, January 19, 2011.

[38] U.S. Small Business Administration, "FY2011 Congressional Budget Justification and FY2009 Annual Performance Report," Washington, DC, 2010, p. 56.

[39] U.S. Small Business Administration, *Agency Financial Report, Fiscal Year 2010* (Washington, DC: GPO, 2010), p. 11.

[40] U.S. Small Business Administration, Office of Congressional and Legislative Affairs, correspondence with the author, January 19, 2011.

[41] U.S. Small Business Administration, Office of Entrepreneurial Development, "Impact Study of Entrepreneurial Development Resources," Washington, DC, September 13, 2010, p. 4, http://www.sba.gov/sites/default/files/09-10%20SBA%20ED%20Resources%20Impact%20Study%20Final%20Report.pdf.

[42] Ibid., p. 67.

[43] Ibid., pp. 71-75.

[44] 15 U.S.C. § 636 7(m)(1)(A).

[45] For further analysis of the SBA's Microloan program see CRS Report R41057, *Small Business Administration Microloan Program*, by Robert Jay Dilger.

[46] 15 U.S.C. § 636(m)(4)(A).

[47] 13 C.F.R § 120.712.

[48] Ibid.

[49] 13 C.F.R § 120.712. Intermediaries may not borrow their contribution.

[50] An economically distressed area is a county or equivalent division of local government which, according to the most recent available data from the United States Bureau of the Census, 40% or more of the residents have an annual income that is at or below the poverty level. See 13 C.F.R § 120.701.

[51] 13 C.F.R § 120.712.

[52] Intermediaries that make at least 25% of their loans to small businesses located in or owned by residents of an Economically Distressed Area (defined as having 40% or more of its residents with an annual income that is at or below the poverty level), or have a portfolio of loans made under the program that averages not more than $10,000 during the period of the intermediary's participation in the program are eligible to receive an additional training grant equal to 5% of the total outstanding balance of loans made to the intermediary. Intermediaries are not required to make a matching contribution as a condition of receiving these additional grant funds. See 13 C.F.R § 120.712; and 15 U.S.C. § 636(m)(4)(C)(i).

[53] U.S. Small Business Administration, Office of Congressional and Legislative Affairs, correspondence with the authors, January 14, 2011.

[54] U.S. Small Business Administration, Office of Congressional and Legislative Affairs, correspondence with the authors, January 19, 2011.

[55] U.S. Congress, Senate Select Committee on Small Business, *Small Business Administration - 1965*, 89th Cong., 1st sess., May 19, 1965 (Washington: GPO, 1965), pp. 21, 45; and SCORE (Service Corps of Retired Executives), "Milestones in SCORE History," Washington, DC, http://www.score.org/milestones.html.

[56] U.S. Congress, Senate Select Committee on Small Business and House Select Committee on Small Business, *1966 Federal Handbook for Small Business: A Survey of Small Business Programs in the Federal Government Agencies*, committee print, 89th Cong., 3rd sess., January 31, 1966 (Washington: GPO, 1966), p. 5; and U.S. Congress, House Committee on Small Business, Subcommittee on Rural Development, Entrepreneurship, and Trade, *Subcommittee Hearing on Legislative Initiatives to Modernize SBA's Entrepreneurial Development Programs*, 111th Cong., 1st sess., April 2, 2009 (Washington: GPO, 2009), p. 6.

[57] U.S. Congress, Senate Select Committee on Small Business, *Small Business Act*, 90th Cong., 1st sess., November 22, 1967 (Washington: GPO, 1967), pp. 13, 14.

[58] U.S. Small Business Administration, "FY2011 Congressional Budget Justification and FY2009 Annual Performance Report," Washington, DC, 2010, p. 60.

[59] SCORE (Service Corps of Retired Executives), "About SCORE," Washington, DC, http://www. score.org/ explore_score.html.

[60] U.S. Small Business Administration, *Agency Financial Report, Fiscal Year 2010* (Washington, DC: GPO, 2010), p. 7.

[61] Ibid., p. 11.

[62] U.S. Small Business Administration, Office of Congressional and Legislative Affairs, correspondence with the authors, January 19, 2011.

[63] U.S. Congress, House Committee on Small Business, *Full Committee Hearing on Legislation to Reauthorize and Modernize SBA's Entrepreneurial Development Programs*, 111th Cong., 1st sess., May 6, 2009 (Washington: GPO, 2009), p. 53.

[64] U.S. Small Business Administration, Office of Entrepreneurial Development, "Impact Study of Entrepreneurial Development Resources," Washington, DC, September 13, 2010, p. 55, http://www.sba.gov/sites/default/files/09-10%20SBA%20ED%20Resources%20Impact%20 Study%20Final%20Report.pdf.

[65] Ibid., pp. 59-63.

[66] P.L. 106-102, the Gramm-Leach-Bliley Act, Sec. 173. Establishment of Program.

[67] P.L. 106-102, the Gramm-Leach-Bliley Act, Sec. 173. Establishment of Program and Sec. 175. Qualified Organizations.

[68] P.L. 106-102, the Gramm-Leach-Bliley Act, Sec. 176. Allocation of Assistance; Subgrants.

[69] P.L. 106-102, the Gramm-Leach-Bliley Act, Sec. 174. Uses of Assistance.

[70] U.S. Small Business Administration, "PRIME Program," Washington, DC, http://www.sba. gov/content/prime-program-0.

[71] Ibid.

[72] U.S. Small Business Administration, Office of Financial Assistance, "Program for Investment in Microentrepreneurs Act ("PRIME"): Microenterprise and Technical Assistance Programs to Disadvantaged Entrepreneurs, Fiscal Year 2010," June 2010, Washington, DC, p. 2, http://archive.sba.gov/idc/groups/public/documents/sba_homepage/serv_fa_2010_prime track123.pdf.

[73] Ibid., pp. 2, 8.

[74] 13 C.F.R § 119.8.

[75] Ibid.

[76] U.S. Small Business Administration, "SBA Awards $8 Million in PRIME Grants to Help Micro Entrepreneurs Grow their Businesses and Create Jobs," Washington, DC, October 5, 2010, http://www.sba.gov/about-sba-services/7367/ 5515.

[77] U.S. Small Business Administration, Office of Congressional and Legislative Affairs, correspondence with the author, January 19, 2011.

[78] U.S. Congress, House Committee on Small Business, *Veterans Entrepreneurship and Small Business Development Act of 1999*, report to accompany H.R. 1568, 106th Cong., 1st sess., June 29, 1999, H.Rept. 106-206 (Washington: GPO, 1999), pp. 14, 15.

[79] Ibid.

[80] P.L. 106-50, the Veterans Entrepreneurship and Small Business Development Act of 1999, Sec. 33. National Veterans Business Development Corporation.

[81] U.S. Congress, House Committee on Small Business, *Veterans Entrepreneurship and Small Business Development Act of 1999*, report to accompany H.R. 1568, 106th Cong., 1st sess., June 29, 1999, H.Rept. 106-206 (Washington: GPO, 1999), p. 14.

[82] P.L. 106-50, the Veterans Entrepreneurship and Small Business Development Act of 1999, Sec. 301. Score Program.

[83] Ibid., Sec. 302. Entrepreneurial Assistance.

[84] Ibid.

[85] U.S. Small Business Administration, "FY2011 Congressional Budget Justification and FY2009 Annual Performance Report," Washington, DC, 2010, p. 66.

[86] Ibid.

[87] Ibid., pp. 66, 67.

[88] Ibid., p. 67.

[89] U.S. Small Business Administration, Office of Congressional and Legislative Affairs, correspondence with the author, January 19, 2011.

[90] U.S. Small Business Administration, Office of Veterans Business Development, "Special Program Announcement: Veterans Business Outreach Center Program," Washington, DC, April 2010, p. 1, http://archive.sba.gov/idc/groups/ public/documents/sba_program_office/ ovbd_vboc_prgm_announce2010.pdf.

[91] Ibid., p. 2.

[92] U.S. Small Business Administration, "FY2011 Congressional Budget Justification and FY2009 Annual Performance Report," Washington, DC, 2010, p. 67.

[93] 13 C.F.R. § 124.8-1(b) (1970); and Notes, "Minority Enterprise, Federal Contracting, and the SBA's 8(a) Program: A New Approach to an Old Problem," *Michigan Law Review*, vol. 71, no. 2 (December 1972), pp. 377, 378. For further analysis of the Minority Small Business and Capital Ownership Development Program, also known as the 8(a) program, see CRS Report R40744, *The "8(a) Program" for Small Businesses Owned and Controlled by the Socially and Economically Disadvantaged: Legal Requirements and Issues*, by John R. Luckey and Kate M. Manuel.

[94] 13 C.F.R. § 124.8-1(d) (1970).

[95] 13 C.F.R. § 124.702.

[96] U.S. Small Business Administration, "FY2011 Congressional Budget Justification and FY2009 Annual Performance Report," Washington, DC, 2010, p. 63.

[97] U.S. Small Business Administration, Office of Congressional and Legislative Affairs, correspondence with the author, January 21, 2011.

[98] U.S. Small Business Administration, Office of Congressional and Legislative Affairs, correspondence with the authors, January 19, 2011.

[99] U.S. Congress, House Committee on Small Business, Subcommittee on Workforce, Empowerment, and Government Programs, *Oversight of the Small Business Administration's Entrepreneurial Development Programs*, 109th Cong., 2nd sess., March 2, 2006, Serial No. 109-40 (Washington: GPO, 2006), pp. 5, 37. H.R. 2352, the Job Creation Through Entrepreneurship Act of 2009, would provide statutory authorization for the Office of Native American Affairs. It was passed by the House on May 20, 2009.

[100] U.S. Small Business Administration, "FY2011 Congressional Budget Justification and FY2009 Annual Performance Report," Washington, DC, 2010, p. 65.

[101] Ibid.

[102] Ibid.

[103] Ibid.

[104] U.S. Small Business Administration, Office of Congressional and Legislative Affairs, correspondence with the authors, July 16, 2010.

[105] U.S. Small Business Administration, Office of Congressional and Legislative Affairs, correspondence with the authors, January 19, 2011.

[106] U.S. Department of Commerce, Minority Business Development Agency, *Annual Performance Report, Fiscal Year 2008*, Washington, DC, 2009, p. 6, http://www.mbda. gov/?section_id=2&bucket_id=643&content_id=3205&well=entire_page&portal_ document_download=true&download_cid=3205&name=MBDA_Annual_Performance_ Report_2008.pdf&legacy_flag=false.

[107] 13 C.F.R. § 306.

[108] The Executive Office of the President, "Executive Order 11625," 36 *Federal Register* 11625, October 14, 1971; and 3 C.F.R., 1971-1975 Comp. 9. 616. The MBDA superseded the Office of Minority Business Enterprise, which was established by Executive Order 11458 signed by President Richard Nixon on March 5, 1969.

[109] U.S. Department of Commerce Minority Business Development Agency, *Annual Performance Report, Fiscal Year 2008*, Washington, DC, 2009, p. 14, http://www.mbda.gov/?section_id=2&bucket_id=643&content_id=3205&well=entire_page&portal_document_download=true&download_cid=3205&name=MBDA_Annual_Performance_Report_2008.pdf&legacy_flag=false.

[110] In addition, since 1970, Congress has periodically allocated supplemental funds for EDA to assist with disaster mitigation and economic recovery. Also, EDA grant applicants must be designated by EDA as part of an EDD—a multijurisdictional consortium of county and local governments—to be eligible for EDA funding and grants. To be designated as an EDD, an area must meet the definition of economic distress, under 13 C.F.R 303.3: (i) An unemployment rate that is, for the most recent twenty-four (24) month period for which data are available, at least one (1) percentage point greater than the national average unemployment rate; (ii) Per capita income that is, for the most recent period for which data are available, eighty (80) percent or less of the national average per capita income; or (iii) A Special Need, as determined by Economic Development Administration (EDA).

[111] 13 C.F.R. § 306.

[112] U.S. Congress, House Committee on Small Business, *Full Committee Markup of H.R. 2352 The Job Creation Through Entrepreneurship Act of 2009*, 111th Cong., 1st sess., May 13, 2009, Doc. No. 111-022 (Washington: GPO, 2009), pp. 2, 14; U.S. Congress, Senate Committee on Small Business, *SBA's Management and Assistance Programs*, Roundtable before the Committee on Small Business United States Senate, 106th Cong., 1st sess., May 20, 1999, S. Hrg. 106-337 (Washington: GPO, 1999), pp. 69, 74, 82, 92; U.S. Congress, House Committee on Small Business, *To Investigate the Legislation That Would Increase the Extent and Scope of the Services Provided By Small Business Development Centers*, 107th Cong., 1st sess., July 19, 2001, Serial No. 107-20 (Washington: GPO, 2001), pp. 13, 59, 60; and U.S. Congress, Senate Committee on Small Business, *Oversight on the Small Business Administration's Small Business Development Center Program*, 100th Cong., 1st sess., October 15, 1987, S. Hrg. 100-339 (Washington: GPO, 1987), pp. 6, 165, 168, 230.

[113] Representative Sam Graves, "Opening Statement for Views and Estimates Markup," Washington, DC, March 15, 2011, http://www.smallbusiness.house.gov/Calendar/EventSingle.aspx?EventID=227626.

[114] U.S. Congress, House Committee on Small Business, "Views and Estimates of the Committee on Small Business on Matters to be set forth in the Concurrent Resolution on the Budget for FY2012, communication to the Chairman, House Committee on the Budget," 112th Cong., 1st sess., March 17, 2011, http://smbiz.house.gov/UploadedFiles/March_17_Views_and_Estimates_Letter.pdf.

[115] U.S. Congress, House Committee on Small Business, *Full Committee Hearing on Legislation to Reauthorize and Modernize SBA's Entrepreneurial Development Programs*, 111th Cong., 1st sess., May 6, 2009 (Washington: GPO, 2009), pp. 12, 13, 15, 18.

[116] U.S. Government Accountability Office, Small Business Administration: Opportunities Exist to Improve Oversight of Women's Business Centers and Coordination among SBA's Business Assistance Programs, GAO-08-49, November 2007, pp. 6, 24-31, http://www.gao.gov/new.items/d0849.pdf.

[117] U.S. Congress, House Committee on Small Business, *Full Committee Hearing on the State of the SBA's Entrepreneurial Development Programs and Their Role in Promoting an Economic Recovery*, 111th Cong., 1st sess., February 11, 2009, Small Business Comm. Doc. No. 111-005 (Washington: GPO, 2009), p. 4.

[118] U.S. Congress, House Committee on Small Business, Subcommittee on Rural Development, Entrepreneurship, and Trade, *Subcommittee Hearing on Legislative Initiatives to Modernize SBA's Entrepreneurial Development Programs*, 111th Cong., 1st sess., April 2, 2009 (Washington: GPO, 2009), p. 29.

[119] U.S. Congress, House Committee on Small Business, *Full Committee Hearing on the State of the SBA's Entrepreneurial Development Programs and Their Role in Promoting an*

Economic Recovery, 111th Cong., 1st sess., February 11, 2009, Small Business Committee Doc. No. 111-005 (Washington: GPO, 2009), p. 26.

[120] Ibid., pp. 15, 17, 26, 29, 58-65, 72; and U.S. Congress, House Committee on Small Business, *Women's Business Ownership Act of 1988*, report to accompany H.R. 5050, 100th Cong., 2nd sess., September 22, 1988, H.Rept. 100-955 (Washington: GPO, 1988), pp. 9, 10, 13, 14.

[121] U.S. Congress, House Committee on Small Business, *Full Committee Legislative Hearing on Energy, Veterans Entrepreneurship, and the SBA's Entrepreneurial Development Programs*, 110th Cong., 1st sess., May 16, 2007, Serial Number 110-22 (Washington: GPO, 2007), p. 20.

[122] U.S. Congress, House Committee on Small Business, *Full Committee Hearing on the State of the SBA's Entrepreneurial Development Programs and Their Role in Promoting an Economic Recovery*, 111th Cong., 1st sess., February 11, 2009, Small Business Committee Doc. No. 111-005 (Washington: GPO, 2009), pp. 45, 47.

[123] U.S. Congress, House Committee on Small Business, *Job Creation Through Entrepreneurship Act of 2009*, report to accompany H.R. 2352, 111th Cong., 1st sess., May 15, 2009, H.Rept. 111-112 (Washington: GPO, 2009), pp. 17, 18.

[124] H.R. 2352, the Job Creation Through Entrepreneurship Act of 2009, Sec. 201. Educating Entrepreneurs Through Technology; and H.R. 2352, the Job Creation Through Entrepreneurship Act of 2009, Sec. 601. Expanding Entrepreneurship.

[125] H.R. 2352, the Job Creation Through Entrepreneurship Act of 2009, Sec. 601. Expanding Entrepreneurship.

[126] Ibid.

[127] U.S. Government Accountability Office, Small Business Administration: Opportunities Exist to Improve Oversight of Women's Business Centers and Coordination among SBA's Business Assistance Programs, GAO-08-49, November 2007, p. 15, http://www.gao.gov/new.items/d0849.pdf.

[128] Ibid.

[129] U.S. Small Business Administration, "FY/CY 2011, Program Announcement for Renewal of the Cooperative Agreement for Current Recipient Organizations," Washington, DC, pp. 27-38, http://ohiosbdcifp.com/Documents/ 12%20Program%20Announcement%20FFY2011%20DRAFT%20.pdf.

[130] H.R. 2352, the Job Creation Through Entrepreneurship Act of 2009, Sec. 404. Performance and Planning.

[131] H.R. 2352, the Job Creation Through Entrepreneurship Act of 2009, Sec. 601. Expanding Entrepreneurship.

[132] U.S. Congress, House Committee on Small Business, Subcommittee on Rural Development, Entrepreneurship and Trade, *Subcommittee Hearing on Legislative Initiatives to Modernize SBA's Entrepreneurial Development Programs*, 111th Cong., 1st sess., April 2, 2009, H. Hrg. 111-015 (Washington: GPO, 2009), pp. 26, 27, 31.

[133] U.S. Congress, House Committee on Small Business, Subcommittee on Rural and Urban Entrepreneurship, *Subcommittee Hearing on Oversight of the Entrepreneurial Development Programs Implemented By the Small Business Administration and National Veterans Business Development Corporation*, 110th Cong., 2nd sess., March 12, 2008, House Serial No. 110-78 (Washington: GPO, 2008), pp. 17, 18.

[134] In addition to authorizing changes to the SBA's loan guaranty, training, and contracting programs, the Small Business Jobs Act of 2010 authorizes a $30 billion Small Business Lending Fund to encourage community banks to provide small business loans, a $1.5 billion State Small Business Credit Initiative to provide funding to participating states with small business capital access programs, and about $12 billion in tax relief for small businesses. It also includes revenue raising provisions to offset the act's cost. For further analysis see CRS Report R41385, *Small Business Legislation During the 111th Congress*, by Robert Jay Dilger, Oscar R. Gonzales, and Gary Guenther.

[135] P.L. 111-240, the Small Business Jobs Act of 2010, Sec. 1401. Matching Requirements Under Small Business Programs. This provision was also included in S. 3165, Small Business Community Partner Relief Act of 2010; and a similar provision was included in S. 3103, the Small Business Job Creation Act of 2010.

[136] Ibid.

[137] The bill would also establish a Rural Small Business Technology Pilot Program, increase maximum loan limits for the SBA's home and business disaster loan programs, increase surety bond limits, and expand eligibility for the SBA's State Trade and Export Promotion Grant Program to cities and other major metropolitan areas.

[138] S. 3967, the Small Business Investment and Innovation Act of 2010, Sec. 241. Office of Women's Business Ownership.

[139] U.S. Small Business Administration, Office of Advocacy, *Small Business Economic Indicators for 2003*, Washington, DC, August 2004, p. 3; Brian Headd, "Small Businesses Most Likely to Lead Economic Recovery," *The Small Business Advocate*, vol. 28, no. 6 (July 2009), pp. 1, 2; and U.S. Small Business Administration, *Fiscal Year 2010 Congressional Budget Justification* (Washington: GPO, 2009), p. 1.

[140] U.S. Congress, House Committee on Small Business, Subcommittee on Rural Development, Entrepreneurship and Trade, *Subcommittee On Rural Development, Entrepreneurship And Trade Markup On Entrepreneurial Development Programs Legislation*, 111th Cong., 1st sess., April 30, 2009, Small Business Committee Document No. 111-118 [ERRATA – printing error, should be 111-018] (Washington: GPO, 2009), p. 1.

[141] David Port, "But Where Is the Money?" *Entrepreneur Magazine*, August 2010, *http://www. entrepreneur.com/ magazine/entrepreneur/2010/august/207500.html*.

[142] U.S. Congress, House Committee on Small Business, *Full Committee Hearing on the State of the SBA's Entrepreneurial Development Programs and Their Role in Promoting an Economic Recovery*, 111th Cong., 1st sess., February 11, 2009, Small Business Committee Doc. No. 111-005 (Washington: GPO, 2009), pp. 3-5, 24-27, 29; and U.S. Congress, House Committee on Small Business, *Full Committee Hearing on Legislation to Reauthorize and Modernize SBA's Entrepreneurial Development Programs*, 111th Cong., 1st sess., May 6, 2009 (Washington: GPO, 2009), pp. 3-5, 15, 27-34.

[143] U.S. Congress, House Committee on Small Business, *Full Committee Hearing on the State of the SBA's Entrepreneurial Development Programs and Their Role in Promoting an Economic Recovery*, 111th Cong., 1st sess., February 11, 2009, Small Business Committee Doc. No. 111-005 (Washington: GPO, 2009), pp. 44-49; U.S. Congress, House Committee on Small Business, *Job Creation Through Entrepreneurship Act of 2009*, report to accompany H.R. 2352, 111th Cong., 1st sess., May 15, 2009, H.Rept. 111-112 (Washington: GPO, 2009), pp. 16-31; and U.S. Congress, House Committee on Small Business, *Women's Business Ownership Act of 1988*, report to accompany H.R. 5050, 100th Cong., 2nd sess., September 22, 1988, H.Rept. 100-955 (Washington: GPO, 1988), pp. 9, 10, 13, 14.

In: Small Business Assistance
Editors: Patrick J. Walker

ISBN: 978-1-62100- 707-4
© 2012 Nova Science Publishers, Inc.

Chapter 2

SBA SMALL BUSINESS INVESTMENT COMPANY PROGRAM

Robert Jay Dilger and Oscar R. Gonzales

SUMMARY

The Small Business Administration (SBA) administers several programs to support small businesses, including loan guaranty programs to enhance small business access to capital; programs to increase small business opportunities in federal contracting; direct loans for businesses, homeowners, and renters to assist their recovery from natural disasters; and access to entrepreneurial education to assist with business formation and expansion. It also administers the Small Business Investment Company (SBIC) Program. Authorized by P.L. 85-699, the Small Business Investment Act of 1958, as amended, the SBIC program enhances small business access to venture capital by stimulating and supplementing "the flow of private equity capital and long term loan funds which small business concerns need for the sound financing of their business operations and for their growth, expansion, and modernization, and which are not available in adequate supply." Facilitating the flow of capital to small businesses to stimulate the national economy was, and remains, the SBIC program's primary objective.

The SBA does not make direct investments in small businesses. It works with 302 privately owned and managed SBICs licensed by the SBA to provide financing to small businesses with private capital the SBIC has raised and with funds the SBIC borrows at favorable rates because the SBA guarantees the debenture (loan obligation).

SBICs pursue investments in a broad range of industries, geographies, and stage of investment. Some SBICs specialize in a particular field or industry in which their management has expertise, while others invest more generally. Most SBICs concentrate on a particular stage of investment (i.e., start-up, expansion, or turnaround) and identify a geographic area in which to focus.

The SBIC program currently has invested about $15.0 billion in small businesses, with about $8.8 billion raised from private capital and $6.2 billion guaranteed by the SBA. In FY2010, the SBA guaranteed $931 million in SBIC small business investments, and SBICs provided another $1.1 billion in investments from private capital, for a total of more than $2.0 billion in financing for 1,331 small businesses.

Congressional interest in the SBIC program has increased in recent years primarily because it is viewed as a means to stimulate economic activity, create jobs, and assist in the national economic recovery. However, there are disagreements concerning whether the program should target additional assistance to startup and early-stage small businesses, which are generally viewed as relatively risky investments but also as having a relatively high potential for job creation.

This report examines the SBIC program's structure and operation, focusing on SBIC eligibility requirements, investment activity, and program statistics. It also examines legislation considered during the 111th Congress, including H.R. 3854, the Small Business Financing and Investment Act of 2009, H.R. 5554, the Small Business Assistance and Relief Act of 2010, and P.L. 111-240, the Small Business Jobs Act of 2010, which address the following SBIC-related issues: (1) the targeting of additional assistance to startup and early-stage small businesses, (2) the SBA's management of the program's financial risk and its processing of SBIC applications, and (3) whether the program's financing levels are appropriate given the nation's current economic circumstances.

SBIC Program Overview

The Small Business Administration (SBA) administers several programs to support small businesses, including loan guaranty programs to enhance small business access to capital; programs to increase small business opportunities in federal contracting; direct loans for businesses, homeowners, and renters to assist their recovery from natural disasters; and access to entrepreneurial education to assist with business formation and expansion.[1] It also administers the Small Business Investment Company (SBIC) Program. Authorized by P.L. 85-699, the Small Business Investment Act of 1958, as amended, the SBIC program enhances small business access to venture capital by stimulating and supplementing "the flow of private equity capital and long term loan funds which small business concerns need for the sound financing of their business operations and for their growth, expansion, and modernization, and which are not available in adequate supply."[2]

The SBIC program was created to address concerns raised in a Federal Reserve Board report to Congress that concluded that a gap existed in the capital markets for long-term funding for growth-oriented small businesses. The report noted that the SBA's loan programs were "limited to providing short-term and intermediate-term credit when such loans are unavailable from private institutions," and the SBA "did not provide equity financing."[3] Equity financing (or equity capital) is money raised by a company in exchange for a share of ownership in the business. Ownership is represented by owning shares of stock outright or having the right to convert other financial instruments into stock. Equity financing allows a business to obtain funds without incurring debt, or without having to repay a specific amount of money at a particular time. The Federal Reserve Board's report concluded that there was a need for a federal government program to "stimulate the availability of capital funds to small business" to assist them in gaining access to long-term financing and equity financing.[4] Facilitating the flow of capital to small businesses to stimulate the national economy was, and remains, the SBIC program's primary objective.

The SBA does not make direct investments in small businesses. It works with 302 privately owned and managed SBICs licensed by the SBA to provide financing to small businesses with private capital the SBIC has raised and with funds the SBIC borrows at favorable rates because the SBA guarantees the debenture (loan obligation).

Congressional interest in the SBIC program has increased in recent years primarily because it is viewed as another means to stimulate economic activity, create jobs, and assist in the national economic recovery. However, there are disagreements concerning whether the program should target additional assistance to startup and early-stage small businesses, which are generally viewed as relatively risky investments but also as having a relatively high potential for job creation.

This report examines the structure and operation of the SBIC program, focusing on SBIC eligibility requirements, investment activity, and program statistics. It also examines legislation, including H.R. 3854, the Small Business Financing and Investment Act of 2009, H.R. 5554, the Small Business Assistance and Relief Act of 2010, and P.L. 111-240, the Small Business Jobs Act of 2010, which address the following SBIC-related issues: (1) the targeting of additional assistance to startup and early-stage small businesses, (2) the SBA's management of the program's financial risk and its processing of SBIC applications, and (3) whether the program's financing levels are appropriate given the nation's current economic circumstances.

SBIC TYPES

There are two types of SBICs. Investment companies licensed under Section 301(c) of the Small Business Investment Act of 1958, as amended, are referred to as original, or regular, SBICs. Investment companies licensed under Section 301(d) of the act, called Specialized Small Business Investment Companies (SSBICs), focus on providing financing to small business entrepreneurs "whose participation in the free enterprise system is hampered because of social or economic disadvantage."[5] Section 301(d) was repealed by P.L. 104-208, the Omnibus Consolidated Appropriations Act, 1997 (Title II of Division D, the Small Business Programs Improvement Act of 1996). As a result, no new SSBIC licenses have been issued since October 1, 1996. However, existing SSBICs were "grandfathered" in and remain in operation.

With few exceptions, SBICs and SSBICs are subject to the same eligibility requirements and operating rules and regulations. Therefore, the SBIC name is usually used to refer to both SBICs and SSBICs simultaneously.

In addition, regular SBICs are also distinguished by the nature of their financings. As will be discussed, there are debenture SBICs, participating securities SBICs, and bank-owned, non-leveraged SBICs. Debentures are debt obligations issued by SBICs and held or guaranteed by the SBA.[6] Participating securities are redeemable, preferred, equity-type securities, often in the form of limited partnership interests, preferred stock, or debentures with interest payable only to the extent of earnings.[7]

SBIC ELIGIBILITY REQUIREMENTS

An SBIC can be organized in any state, as either a corporation, limited partnership (LP), or a limited liability company (LLCs must be organized under Delaware law). Most SBICs are owned by relatively small groups of local investors, although many are partially owned, and some are wholly owned (46 of 302), by commercial banks.[8] A few SBICs are corporations with publicly traded stock.[9]

The two primary criteria for licensure as an SBIC are having qualified management and sufficient private capital. The SBA reviews and approves prospective SBIC's management teams based upon their professional capabilities and character. Specifically, the SBA examines the SBIC's management team looking for

- substantive and relevant principal investment experience;
- realized track record of superior returns, based on an overall evaluation of appropriate quantitative performance measures;
- evidence of a strong rate of business proposals and investment offers (deal flow) in the investment area proposed for the new fund;
- a cohesive management team, with complementary skills and history of working together;
- managerial, operational, or technical experience that can add value at the portfolio company level; and
- a demonstrated ability to manage cash flows so as to provide assurance the SBA will be repaid on a timely basis.[10]

Debenture SBICs are required to have a minimum private capital investment of $5 million (called regulatory capital).[11] The SBA has discretion to license an applicant with regulatory capital of $3 million if the applicant has satisfied all licensing standards and requirements, has a viable business plan reasonably projecting profitable operations, and has a reasonable timetable for achieving regulatory capital of at least $5 million.[12] At least 30% of the debenture SBIC's regulatory and leverageable capital must come from three people unaffiliated with the fund's management and with each other.[13] Also, no more than 33% of the SBIC's regulatory capital can come from state or local government entities.[14]

Participating securities SBICs must have regulatory capital of $10 million. The SBA has discretion to require less than $10 million in regulatory capital if the licensee can demonstrate that it can be financially viable over the long term with a lower amount. In this circumstance, the regulatory amount required can not be lower than $5 million.[15] At least 30% of the participating securities SBIC's regulatory and leverageable capital must come from three people unaffiliated with the fund's management and with each other.[16] Also, no more than 33% of the SBIC's regulatory capital can come from state or local government entities.[17]

The eligibility requirements for small businesses requesting financial assistance from an SBIC is described in the Appendix.

SBIC APPLICATION PROCESS

Applying for an SBIC license is a multi-step process, beginning with the submission of the SBA Management Assessment Questionnaire (MAQ). It includes, among others, questions concerning

- the fund's legal name, and the name and addresses of its principals and control persons;
- the fund's finances and expenses;
- the management team's professional experience;
- the fund's expected investing focus (e.g., will the fund be primarily a sole investor, lead investor, or co-investor; its anticipated percentage of investments in technology, life sciences, health care, manufacturing, distribution, service, consumer products and retail, or other industries; and its anticipated percentage of investments by business life cycle—seed, early stage, expansion, later stage, change of control, or turnaround);
- the geographic areas where the investments are expected to be made;
- the anticipated holding periods for investments;
- the types and characteristics of the securities that will be used to make investments; and
- the extent to which "special groups of businesses" will be targeted for investment, such as "ethnic groups, women, rural, inner city, etc."[18]

After receiving the firm's application a member of the SBA's Program Development Office reviews the MAQ, assesses the investment company's proposal in light of the program's minimum requirements and management qualifications, performs initial due diligence including making reference telephone calls, and prepares a written recommendation to the SBA's Investment Division's Investment Committee (composed of senior members of the Division).

If, after reviewing the MAQ and the SBA's Program Development Office's evaluation, the Investment Committee concludes, by majority vote at a regularly scheduled meeting, that the investment company's management team may be qualified for a license, the investment company's management team is invited to the SBA's headquarters in Washington, DC, for an interview. If, following the interview, the Investment Committee votes to proceed, the investment team is provided a "Green Light" letter, formally inviting the investment team to file a license application, along with a filing fee of $10,000, plus an additional $5,000 for partnerships or LLC SBICs. If the license is approved, all SBIC principals must complete the SBA's SBIC Regulations training classes. On average, obtaining an SBIC license takes about six months from the time of the initial submission of the MAQ to issuance of the license.[19]

The application process for small businesses requesting financial assistance from an SBIC is described in the Appendix.

SBIC INVESTMENT ACTIVITY

SBIC Investments in Small Businesses

SBICs provide equity capital to small businesses in various ways, including by

- purchasing small business equity securities (e.g., stock, stock options, warrants, limited partnership interests, membership interests in a limited liability company, or joint venture interests);[20]
- making loans to small businesses, either independently or in cooperation with other private or public lenders, that have a maturity of no more than 20 years;[21]
- purchasing debt securities from small businesses, which may be convertible into, or have rights to purchase, equity in the small business;[22] and
- subject to limitations, providing small businesses a guarantee of their monetary obligations to creditors not associated with the SBIC.[23]

SBICs are subject to statutory and regulatory restrictions concerning the nature of their approved investments. For example, SBICs are not allowed to

- directly or indirectly provide financing to any of their associates (e.g., officers, directors, and employees);[24]
- control, either directly or indirectly, any small business on a permanent basis;[25]
- invest, without SBA approval, more than specified percentages of its private (regulatory) capital in securities, commitments, or guarantees in any one small business (e.g., SBICs are not allowed to invest more than 30% of their private capital in any one small business if their investment plan includes two or more tiers of SBA leverage);[26]
- invest in farm land, unimproved land, or any small business classified under Major Group 65 (Real Estate) of the Standard Industrial Classification (SIC) Manual, with the exception of title abstract companies, real estate agents, brokers, and managers;[27]
- provide funds for small businesses whose primary business activity involves directly or indirectly providing funds to others, purchasing debt obligations, factoring, or leasing equipment on a long-term basis with no provision for maintenance or repair;[28] or
- provide funds to a small business if the funds will be used substantially for a foreign operation.[29]

The SBA also regulates the interest rates and fees SBICs are allowed to charge small businesses on loans, debt securities, and equity financing.[30]

In 1999, the SBA introduced the low and moderate income investments (LMI) initiative to encourage SBICs to invest in small businesses located in inner cities and rural areas "that have a severe shortages of equity capital" because investments in those areas "often are of a type that will not have the potential for yielding returns that are high enough to justify the use of participating securities."[31] This ongoing initiative provides incentives to SBICs that invest in small businesses that have at least 50% of its employees or tangible assets located in a low-to-moderate income area (LMI Zone) or have at least 35% of its full-time employees with their primary residence in an LMI Zone.[32] For example, unlike regular SBIC debentures that typically have a 10-year maturity, LMI debentures are available in two maturities, for five years and 10 years, plus the stub period. The stub period is the time between the debenture's issuance date and the next March 1 or September 1. The stub period allows all LMI Debentures to have common March 1 or September 1 maturity dates to simplify administration of the program.

In addition, LMI debentures are issued at a discount so that the proceeds the SBIC receives for the sale of the debenture are reduced by (1) the debenture's interest costs for the first five years, plus the stub period; (2) the SBA's annual fee for the debenture's first five years, plus the stub period; and (3) the SBA's 2% leverage fee. As a result, these interest costs and fees are effectively deferred, freeing SBICs from the requirement to make interest payments on LMI debentures, or pay the SBA's annual fees on LMI debentures, for the first five years of the debenture, plus the stub period between the debenture's issuance date and the next March 1 or September 1.[33]

In FY2010, SBICs made 569 financings to small businesses located in a LMI Zone, totaling $444.5 million—about 22% of the total amount financed.[34]

SBA Investments

Leverage

A licensed SBIC in good standing, with a demonstrated need for funds, may apply to the SBA for financial assistance (called leverage) of up to 300% of its private capital. However, most SBICs are approved for a maximum of 200% of its private capital and no fund management team may exceed the allowable maximum amount of leverage, currently $150 million per SBIC and $225 million for two or more licenses under common control.[35] SBICs licensed on or after October 1, 2009, may elect to have a maximum leverage amount of $175 million per SBIC and $250 million for two or more licenses under common control if it has invested at least 50% of its financings in low-income geographic areas and certifies that at least 50% of its future investments will be in low-income geographic areas.[36]

The SBIC's application for SBA financial assistance is to secure the "SBA's conditional commitment to reserve a specific amount of leverage" for the SBIC's future use.[37] If the application is approved, the SBIC draws down the leverage as it makes financial commitments. Leverage is provided through the issuance of either SBA-guaranteed debentures or SBA-guaranteed participating securities.

Debentures

Debenture SBICs obtain leverage by issuing SBA-guaranteed debentures. The SBA pools these debentures and sells SBA-guaranteed debenture participation certificates, representing an undivided interest in the pool, to investors through periodic public offerings.[38] SBA-guaranteed debenture participation certificates can have a term of up to 15 years, although currently only one outstanding SBA-guaranteed debenture participation certificate has a term exceeding 10 years and all recent public offerings have specified a term of 10 years.[39] SBA-guaranteed debentures provide for semi-annual interest payments and a lump sum principal payment to investors at maturity.[40] SBICs are allowed to prepay SBA-guaranteed debentures without penalty. However, a SBA-guaranteed debenture must be prepaid in whole and not in part, and can only be prepaid on a semi-annual payment date. The debenture's coupon (interest) rate is determined by market conditions and the interest rate of 10-year treasury securities at the time of the sale.[41] Also, as mentioned previously, LMI debentures are available in two maturities, for five years and 10 years (plus the stub period).

Because the SBA guarantees the debenture, investors are more likely to purchase the SBIC's debenture participation certificate as opposed to others available on the market. They are also more likely to accept a lower coupon (interest) rate than what would be expected without the SBA's guarantee.[42] As a result, the SBIC's access to venture capital is enhanced, and its cost of raising additional financial resources is reduced. Because debenture SBICs make semi-annual interest payments to investors, they tend to focus their investments on mid- and later-stage small businesses that have positive cash flow and are seeking capital for expansion.[43]

The SBA operates the SBIC debenture program on a zero-subsidy basis. To recoup its expenses, the SBA requires the SBIC to pay a 3% origination fee for each debenture issued (1% at commitment and 2% at draw), an annual fee on the leverage drawn which is fixed at the time of the leverage commitment, and other administrative and underwriting fees which are adjusted annually.[44]

Participating Securities

P.L. 102-366, the Small Business Credit and Business Opportunity Enhancement Act of 1992 (Title IV, the Small Business Equity Enhancement Act of 1992), authorized the SBA to guarantee participating securities. Participating securities are redeemable, preferred, equity-type securities issued by SBICs in the form of limited partnership interests, preferred stock, or debentures with interest payable only to the extent of earnings.

In 1994, the SBA established the SBIC Participating Securities Program (SBIC PSP) to encourage the formation of participating securities SBICs which would make equity investments in startup and early stage small businesses. The SBA created the program to fill a perceived investment gap created by the SBIC debenture program's focus on mid- and later-stage small businesses. As will be discussed, the SBIC PSP lost more than $2.7 billion during the early 2000s. In 2004, the SBA began an ongoing process to end the program. However, in recent years, congressional interest in either revising the program or starting a new program modeled on certain aspects of the SBIC PSP to assist startup and early-stage small businesses has increased.[45]

Participating securities SBICs obtained leverage by issuing SBA-guaranteed participating securities. The SBA pooled these participating securities and sold SBA-guaranteed participating securities certificates, representing an undivided interest in the pool, to investors through periodic public offerings. The SBA's regulations allow these certificates to have a term of up to 15 years, but all recent public offerings have specified a term of 10 years.

There have been 35 public offerings of SBA-guaranteed participating securities certificates since the start of the participating securities program, amounting to just under $10.3 billion. The final SBA-guaranteed participating securities certificate, for $332 million, had a term of 10 years and was offered to investors on February 19, 2009.[46]

SBIC participating securities certificates provide for quarterly payments to investors from dividends on preferred stock, interest on an income bond, or a priority return on a preferred limited partnership equal to a specified interest rate on the principal amount and a lump sum principal payment at maturity. The participating securities SBIC is obligated to make these quarterly payments "only to the extent it has sufficient profits available to make such payments."[47] If it is unable to make any required payment, the SBA will make the payment on behalf of the SBIC. Because startup and early-stage small businesses often are not initially profitable, the SBA included language in its participating securities' offering circulars that it "anticipates that it will be called upon routinely to make such ... payments for the SBICs in the early years of the lives of such SBICs" and that it "expects to be reimbursed [by the SBIC] any amounts paid ... under its guarantee over the life of a participating security."[48]

Because the SBA guaranteed the certificate, investors were more likely to purchase the SBIC's participating securities certificate as opposed to others available on the market. They were also more likely to accept a lower payment rate than what would be expected without the SBA's guarantee.[49]

In addition, participating securities SBICs are more likely than debenture SBICs to finance startup and early-stage small businesses because the SBA is willing to make the SBIC's required quarterly payments to investors, at least during the early years of the investment. Because participating securities SBICs are not required to make these quarterly payments, they are encouraged to focus on the small business's long-term prospects for growth and profitability, rather than on its prospects for having immediate positive cash-flow.[50]

In 2004, the SBA projected losses of more than $2.7 billion in the SBIC PSP, primarily because investments in technology startup and early-stage small businesses lost much of their stock value during the early 2000s. Consequently, on October 1, 2004, the SBA ceased issuing new licenses and new leverage for participating securities SBICs, effectively beginning the process of ending the SBIC PSP.[51] The SBA continued to honor its existing commitments to participating securities SBICs and they were allowed to continue operations. However, they were required to comply with special rules concerning minimum capital, liquidity, non-SBA borrowing, and equity investing.[52] As mentioned previously, the final SBA-guaranteed participating securities participation certificate was offered to investors on February 19, 2009.[53]

As of May 31, 2011, the SBA had a guarantee on the outstanding unpaid principal balance of $4.0 billion in SBIC debentures, $2.4 billion in SBIC participating securities, and $14.0 million in SSBIC financings.[54]

Reporting Requirements

Once licensed, each SBIC is required to file with the SBA an annual financial report which includes an audit by an SBA-approved independent public accountant. SBICs are also subject to annual onsite regulatory compliance examinations.[55] SBICs are also required to provide the SBA:

- a portfolio financing report within 30 days of the closing date for each financing of a small business;[56]
- the value of its loans and investments within 90 days of the end of the fiscal year in the case of annual valuations, and within 30 days following the close of other reporting periods;[57]
- any material adverse changes in valuations at least quarterly (within 30 days following the close of the quarter);[58] and
- copies of reports provided to investors, documents filed with the Securities and Exchange Commission, and documents pertaining to

litigation or other legal proceedings, including criminal charges against any person who was required by the SBA complete a personal history statement in connection with the SBIC's license.[59]

SBIC Program Statistics

There are 302 licensed SBICs in operation (142 debenture SBICs, 101 participating securities SBICs, 46 bank-owned/non-leveraged SBICs, and 13 SSBICs).[60] In FY2010, 218 SBICs provided at least one new financing to a small business.[61]

The number of licensed SBICs has declined in recent years, with most of the decline due to the planned phase-out of participating securities SBICs and SSBICs.[62] For example, in FY2006, there were 396 licensed SBICs (132 debenture SBICs, 173 participating securities SBICs, 67 bank-owned/non-leveraged SBICs, and 24 SSBICs).[63]

Overall, SBICs pursue investments in a broad range of industries, geographies, and stage of investment. Some individual SBICs specialize in a particular field or industry in which their management has expertise, while others invest more generally. Most SBICs concentrate on a particular stage of investment (i.e., start-up, expansion, or turnaround) and identify a geographic area in which to focus.

Total Financing

Since its inception, the SBIC program has provided more than $58.2 billion in financial assistance to more than 107,000 small firms.[64] As mentioned previously, as of May 31, 2011, the SBA had a guarantee on the outstanding unpaid principal balance of $4.0 billion in SBIC debentures, $2.4 billion in SBIC participating securities, and $14.0 million in SSBIC financings.[65] All together, the SBIC program currently has invested about $15.0 billion in small businesses, with about $8.8 billion raised from private capital and $6.2 billion guaranteed by the SBA.[66]

In FY2010, SBICs made 2,455 financings (including 43 financings by SSBICs). The average financing amount was $833,862 ($1,080,295 for debenture SBICs, $420,613 for participating securities SBICs, $838,478 for bank-owned/non-leveraged SBICs, and $68,585 for SSBICs).[67] The funds were used primarily for operating capital (93.3%). Other uses were for research and development (2.8%), to acquire an existing business (1.6%), plant modernization (0.6%), purchasing equipment (0.4%), refinancing or refunding debt (0.3%), marketing activities (0.2%), a new building or plant construction (0.1%), and other uses (0.7%).[68]

As shown in Table 1, the SBA's leverage increased each fiscal year from FY2005 to FY2008, peaking at just over $1.0 billion, declined in FY2009 to $787 million, and increased to $931 million in FY2010. In addition, SBICs provided total investments of more than $2.0 billion in FY2010 ($931 million in SBA leverage and $1.1 billion from private capital), about $1.85 billion in FY2009 ($787 in SBA leverage and $1.06 billion from private capital) and $2.2 billion in FY2008 ($1.0 billion in SBA leverage and $1.2 billion from private capital).[69]

The SBA has had congressional authorization to issue up to $3.0 billion in SBIC leverage each year since 2005. For comparative purposes, private venture capital firms invested $18.3 billion in 2,927 companies in 2009, and $21.8 billion in 3,276 companies in 2010.[70]

The SBA has indicated that one of its goals is "to enhance program acceptance in the marketplace and increase the number of funds licensed and the amount of leverage issued so as to improve capital access for small businesses."[71]

In 2008, the Urban Institute released an analysis comparing debenture SBIC investments made from 1997 to 2005 to private sector venture capital investments made during that time period in second stage business loans, third stage business loans, and bridge loans "because these investments are likely to be of the same character (debt with equity features) as those made by debenture SBICs."[72] The Urban Institute found that debenture SBIC investments accounted for more than 62% of all venture capital financings in second stage business loans, third stage business loans, and bridge loans in the United States during that time period. However, because the average amount of an SBIC debenture investment was much smaller than the industry average, SBIC debenture investments accounted for "only 8% of total dollars invested."[73]

Financing to Specific Demographic Groups

As shown in Table 2, in FY2010, SBICs made 123 financings (5.0% of all financings) amounting to $69.2 million (3.4% of the total amount of financings) to minority-owned and -controlled small businesses.

Table 1. SBIC Financing, FY2005-FY2010 ($ in millions)

Year	SBA Leverage/Guarantee	# of Small Businesses Financed
FY2010	$931	1,331
FY2009	$787	1,481
FY2008	$1,029	1,905
FY2007	$707	2,057
FY2006	$477	1,488
FY2005	$355	1,559

Source: U.S. Small Business Administration, Office of Legislative Affairs, correspondence with the author, October 20, 2010; U.S. Small Business Administration, "Fiscal Year 2011 Congressional Budget Justification and FY2009 Annual Performance Report," Washington, DC, 2010, pp. 19, 51; U.S. Small Business Administration, "FY2010 Congressional Budget Justification," Washington, DC, 2009, pp. 17, 41, 42; U.S. Small Business Administration, "Fiscal Year 2009 Congressional Submission and FY2007 Annual Performance Report," Washington, DC, 2008, pp. 25, 43; U.S. Small Business Administration, "FY 2008 Budget Request and Performance Plan," Washington, DC, 2007, pp. 23, 57; and U.S. Small Business Administration, "Performance and Financial Highlights, FY2007," Washington, DC, February 4, 2008, p. 4.

Table 2. SBIC Financing, Minority-Owned Small Businesses, FY2010

Small Business Ownership Demographic	# of Financings	% of Financings	$ Amount of Financings	% of Total $ Amount of Financings
Black-Owned	40	1.6%	$36,865,781	1.8%
Subcontinent Asian-Owned	39	1.6%	$5,135,745	0.3%
Hispanic-Owned	26	1.1%	$5,402,931	0.3%
Asian Pacific-Owned	18	0.7%	$21,794,698	1.1%
Native American-Owned	0	0.0%	$0	0.0%
Subtotal	123	5.0%	$69,199,155	3.4%
Other (non-minority)	2,332	95.0%	$1,977,932,234	96.6%
Total—All Financings	2,455	100.0%	$2,047,131,389	100.0%

Source: U.S. Small Business Administration, "SBIC Program Financing to Small Businesses – Fiscal Year 2010: Demographics of Financed Businesses.," Washington, DC.

Notes: Ownership is defined as owning at least 50% of the small business.

In addition, in FY2010, SBICs made 43 financings (1.8% of all financings) amounting to $2.1 million (1.4% of the total amount of financings) to women-owned small businesses, and 4 financings (0.2% of all financings) amounting to $1.6 million (0.1% of the total amount of financings) to veteran-owned small businesses.[74]

Research concerning private venture capital investment in minority-owned or women-owned small businesses is limited. As a result, it is difficult to find the data necessary to compare the SBIC program's investment in minority-owned or women-owned small businesses to the private sector's investment in these firms.[75]

In 2007, the SBA acknowledged at a congressional hearing on the SBA's investment programs that "women and minority representation in [the SBIC program] is low" and has been low for many years.[76] The SBA reported at that time that it does not control the investments made by SBICs, but it has tried to increase women and minority representation in the SBIC program by reaching out to venture capital firms, trade organizations, and others to better understand why women and minority representation in the SBIC program is low, and by "finding debenture firms with minority representation on their investment committees and in senior management."[77] However, despite these efforts, in 2009, the National Association of Small Business Investment Companies (NASBIC) asserted at a congressional hearing on the SBA's capital access programs that the SBA's SBIC licensing process "has done an abysmal job at attracting and licensing funds led by women and minorities."[78]

S. 1831, the Small Business Venture Capital Act of 2009, introduced on October 21, 2009, and referred to the Senate Committee on Small Business and Entrepreneurship, would encourage SBIC investments in women-owned small businesses and socially and economically disadvantaged small business concerns by increasing the amount of leverage available to SBICs that invest at least 50% of their financings in small business concerns owned and controlled by women or socially and economically disadvantaged small business concerns.

Financing by State

As shown on Table 3, in FY2010, SBICs provided financing to small businesses located in 46 states, the District of Columbia, and Puerto Rico, with the most financings taking place in New York (455 financings amounting to $243.2 million) and California (422 financings amounting to $295.2 million).

Table 3. SBIC Financing, By State, FY2010 ($ in millions)

State	# of Financings	Amount of Financings	State	# of Financings	Amount of Financings
Alabama	5	$5.1	Montana	1	$0.1
Alaska	0	$0.0	Nebraska	1	$4.0
Arizona	23	$81.3	Nevada	11	$19.2
Arkansas	2	$1.0	New Hampshire	17	$6.9
California	422	$295.2	New Jersey	146	$104.0
Colorado	47	$26.2	New Mexico	5	$0.5
Connecticut	27	$21.3	New York	455	$243.2
Delaware	5	$0.7	North Carolina	61	$70.1
District of Columbia	8	$4.5	North Dakota	3	$8.1
Florida	97	$190.0	Ohio	47	$45.9
Georgia	40	$47.0	Oklahoma	4	$1.9
Hawaii	1	$6.9	Oregon	10	$8.9
Idaho	4	$0.4	Pennsylvania	101	$86.7
Illinois	86	$45.1	Puerto Rico	0	$0.0
Indiana	27	$8.4	Rhode Island	0	$0.0
Iowa	18	$5.4	South Carolina	19	$41.1
Kansas	18	$19.5	South Dakota	0	$0.0
Kentucky	12	$15.7	Tennessee	22	$31.7
Louisiana	5	$10.6	Texas	177	$211.1
Maine	3	$0.5	Utah	37	$23.3
Maryland	25	$13.4	Vermont	15	$20.9
Massachusetts	185	$121.5	Virginia	58	$60.6
Michigan	14	$26.7	Washington	64	$26.6
Minnesota	26	$17.3	West Virginia	11	$2.0
Mississippi	6	$4.3	Wisconsin	35	$25.5
Missouri	49	$37.4	Wyoming	0	$0.0
Total				2,455	$2,047.1

Source: U.S. Small Business Administration, "SBIC Program Financing to Small Businesses – Fiscal Year 2010: SBIC Program Financing by State," Washington, DC.

The previously mentioned 2008 Urban Institute comparative analysis of debenture SBIC financing from 1997 to 2005 found that the dollar volume of investments from debenture SBICs was much more evenly distributed across the nation than from comparable private venture capital funds. For example, the Urban Institute found that California (45.8%) and Massachusetts (12.9%) received the largest share of the total dollar volume invested by private venture capital funds from 1997 to 2005. The two states accounted for more than half (58.7%) of the total dollar volume invested by private venture capital funds. In contrast, New York (18.7%) and California (11.1%) received the largest share of the total dollar volume invested by debenture SBICs from 1997 to 2005. The two states accounted for less than one-third (29.8%) of the total dollar volume invested by debenture SBICs. Also, the top 10 states in terms of their share of the total dollar volume invested accounted nearly 84% of the total invested by private venture capital funds, compared to 64% for debenture SBICs.[79]

Data concerning private sector venture capital fund investments during the third quarter of 2010 and the state-by-state distribution of SBIC financings shown on Table 3 suggest that the Urban Institute's finding that SBICs investments were much more evenly distributed across the nation than private sector venture capital fund investments from 1997 to 2005 may continue to be the case today.[80] For example, California (46.0%) and Massachusetts (10.1%) received the largest share of the total dollar volume invested by private venture capital funds during the third quarter of 2010. The two states accounted for 56.1% of the total dollar volume invested by private venture capital funds. In contrast, California (14.4%) and New York (11.9%) received the largest share of the total dollar volume invested by SBICs during FY2010. The two states accounted for 26.3% of the total dollar volume invested by SBICs.

Financing by Industry

As shown on Table 4, in FY2010, SBIC financings were made in a variety of industries, led by investments in manufacturing; transportation and warehousing; professional, scientific, and technical services; and information.

The previously mentioned 2008 Urban Institute comparative analysis of SBIC financings from 1997 to 2005 found that "SBIC financing is less concentrated by industry than financing from private venture capital firms" and "total financings by SBICs are much less likely to be in hightech industries" than comparable private sector venture capital investment firms.[81]

The Urban Institute found that unlike SBICs, "the value of investments by private venture capital firms is predominately directed towards information and finance," with computer and Internet firms receiving roughly half of all private sector investments.[82]

Table 4. SBIC Financing, By Industry, FY2010

Industry	# of Financings	% of Financings	$ Amount of Financings	% of $ Amount of Financings
Manufacturing	739	30.1%	$527,277,437	25.8%
Transportation and Warehousing	421	17.2%	$217,787,008	10.6%
Professional, Scientific, and Technical Services	333	13.6%	$232,320,253	11.3%
Information	332	13.5%	$236,968,531	11.6%
Wholesale Trade	86	3.5%	$130,427,351	6.4%
Administrative and Support and Waste Management	84	3.4%	$112,767,605	5.5%
Retail Trade	83	3.4%	$71,012,876	3.5%
Accommodation and Food Services	64	2.6%	$29,759,323	1.5%
Health Care and Social Assistance	59	2.4%	$188,706,225	9.2%
Real Estate and Rental Leasing	52	2.1%	$55,785,086	2.7%
Construction	46	1.9%	$39,610,816	1.9%
Finance and Insurance	40	1.6%	$43,746,936	2.1%
Educational Services	18	0.7%	$109,899,891	5.4%
Arts, Entertainment and Recreation	11	0.5%	$2,933,006	0.1%
Mining	5	0.2%	$1,071,239	0.1%
Other Industries	82	3.3%	$47,057,806	2.3%
Total	2,455	100.0%	$2,047,131,389	100.0%

Source: U.S. Small Business Administration, "SBIC Program Financing to Small Businesses – Fiscal Year 2010: Industrial Classification of the Financed Businesses," Washington, DC.

LEGISLATIVE ACTIVITY

P.L. 111-5, the American Recovery and Reinvestment Act of 2009 (ARRA), included provisions designed to increase the amount of leverage issued under the SBIC program by increasing the maximum amount of leverage available to an individual SBIC to 300% of its private capital, or $150 million, whichever is less; and by increasing the maximum amount of leverage available for two or more licenses under common control to $225 million.[83] It also encouraged SBIC investment in smaller enterprises by requiring SBICs licensed on or after the date of its enactment (February 17, 2009) to certify that at least 25% of all future financing dollars are invested in smaller enterprises. ARRA defined smaller enterprises as firms having either a net worth of no more than $6 million and average after-tax net income for the preceding two years of no more than $2 million, or meeting the SBA's size standard for its industry classification.[84]

ARRA also encouraged SBIC investments in low-income areas by allowing SBICs licensed on or after October 1, 2009, to elect to have a maximum leverage amount of $175 million per SBIC and $250 million for two or more licenses under common control if it has invested at least 50% of its financings in low-income geographic areas and certifies that at least 50% of its future investments will be in low-income geographic areas.[85]

Congress also considered several bills during the 111th Congress that were designed to address several other SBIC-related issues, including (1) the targeting of additional assistance to startup and early-stage small businesses, (2) the SBA's management of the program's financial risk and its processing of SBIC license applications, and (3) whether the program's financing levels are appropriate given the nation's current economic circumstances.

Legislation to Target Additional Assistance to Startup and Early-Stage Small Businesses

As mentioned previously, congressional interest in the SBIC program has increased in recent years primarily because it is viewed as a means to stimulate economic activity, create jobs, and assist in the national economic recovery. However, there are disagreements concerning whether the program should target additional assistance to startup and early-stage small businesses, which are generally viewed as relatively risky investments but also as having a relatively high potential for job creation.

Advocates of targeting additional assistance to startup and early-stage small businesses argue that the SBA's participating securities program was created to fill a perceived investment gap resulting from the SBA's debenture program's focus on mid- and later-stage small businesses. Because the SBA is no longer providing new licenses or leverage for participating securities SBICs, they have introduced legislation to create a new SBA program that would focus on the investment needs of startup and early-stage small businesses.

For example, during the 111th Congress the House passed, by a vote of 241-182, H.R. 5297, the Small Business Jobs and Credit Act of 2010. It would have authorized a $1 billion Small Business Early-Stage Investment Program.[86] The proposed program, which was not included in the final version of the bill, which became P.L. 111-240, the Small Business Jobs Act of 2010, would have provided equity investment financing of up to $100 million in matching funds to each participating investment company. It would have required participating investment companies to invest in small businesses, with at least 50% of the financing in early-stage small businesses, defined as not having "gross annual sales revenues exceeding $15 million in any of the previous three years."[87] The proposed program emphasized venture capital investments in start-up companies operating in nine targeted industries.[88]

P.L. 111-240, which was signed into law by President Obama on September 27, 2010, did not include legislative language authorizing a Small Business Early-Stage Investment Program.[89] Instead, it authorizes a three-year Intermediary Lending Pilot Program to provide direct loans to not more than 20 eligible nonprofit lending intermediaries each year, totaling not more than $20 million and $1 million per intermediary. The intermediaries, in turn, can make loans to new or growing small businesses, not to exceed $200,000 per business.[90]

Discussion

Advocates of the Small Business Early-Stage Investment Program and other efforts to encourage capital investment in startup and early-stage small businesses argue that, given the SBA's elimination of the SBIC participating securities program, it is necessary to "fill the gaps in the SBA's existing array of capital access programs, particularly in the provision of capital to early-stage small businesses in capital-intensive industries," because early-stage small businesses "have historically encountered the greatest difficulties in accessing credit."[91] Advocates assert that (1) "these inherent limitations have only been aggravated by the economic downturn;" (2) "venture capital financing and investments in early-stage businesses has stagnated since the last quarter of 2008"; (3) "as a result, the gap for investment in early-stage and capital-intensive small businesses has grown wider"; and (4) "this critical component of the small business community has continued to be underserved by existing government programs."[92] They also argue that "according to SBA studies, the total unmet need for early-stage equity financing for small businesses is about $60 billion annually."[93]

Opponents argue that the Small Business Early-Stage Investment Program "will pile unnecessary risk or costs onto taxpayers at a time when we're dealing with record debt and unsustainable deficit spending."[94] They also argue that the program is untested, that the availability of federal funding is likely to encourage risky investments, and the legislation requires "only 50% of the funding ... to be invested" in early-stage small businesses.[95]

Legislation to Require Expedited SBIC Licensing Procedures

In 2003, the SBA's Office of the Inspector General (OIG) reported that "an ongoing audit of SBIC oversight indicates that policies and procedures in the Investment Division do not limit financial risk."[96] In October 2004, the SBA's OIG issued seven recommendations to reduce the likelihood of the SBA facing large, unanticipated losses in the SBIC program such as those experienced following the collapse of technology-based stock values in 2000 and 2001.[97] Three of the recommendations concerned the SBA's measurement and oversight of potential SBIC program costs and four of the recommendations concerned the oversight and liquidation of financially troubled SBICs.[98]

At that time, the SBA's OIG included the SBA's financial oversight of the SBIC program in its annual list of the most serious management and performance challenges facing the SBA, and indicated that the SBIC program would remain on the list until the recommendations were implemented.[99] In 2009, the SBA's OIG reported that the SBA had adequately addressed five of its seven recommendations.[100] In 2010, the SBA's OIG reported that the SBA had adequately addressed the remaining recommendations and removed the SBIC program from its list of most serious management and performance challenges facing the SBA.[101]

The SBA is currently focusing its attention on improving the SBIC licensing process, which NASBIC has argued in recent congressional hearings is "the number one complaint of SBICs."[102] In FY2009, the SBA took, on average, 13.2 months to process an SBIC license. During the first half of FY2010, the SBA reduced that average processing time to 5.8 months.[103] NASBIC has argued that it should take the SBA no longer than six months, and preferably no longer than four months, to process an application for an SBIC license from a new applicant, and less time than that to process an application for an SBIC license from an existing SBIC.[104]

The SBA reported that it was able to reduce the SBIC licensing processing time in FY2010 by making licensing a priority for the SBA Investment Division, initiating a "Fast Track" licensing process for SBICs seeking a subsequent license, reducing the number of questions asked of SBICs seeking a subsequent license, incorporating timeliness standards in all SBA licensing analysts and supervisors' performance plans to further emphasize speed in processing applications, adding two new analysts to the SBA's licensing office to assist with the processing of applications, and adding another analyst to the SBA's program development office to assist with the review of applications prior to the actual filing of the application.[105] The SBA also reported that is continuing to identify additional processing changes to further "facilitate processing and reduce any redundancies in the process."[106]

Discussion

H.R. 3854, the Small Business Financing and Investment Act of 2009, included a provision requiring the SBA to develop expedited licensing procedures for experienced SBIC applicants. Specifically, the SBA would be required to approve an application for a new SBIC license within 60 days of its receipt if the applicant met a list of requirements, including having been in operation as a licensed SBIC for at least three years prior to the receipt of the request, having at least half of the principal managers of the applicant consist of at least two-thirds of the principal managers of a licensed SBIC, meeting specified minimum performance thresholds (such as having maintained six consecutive quarters of profitable net investment income and at least three exits from investments in small businesses that have realized profits from those respective investments), and being in good standing.[107] The bill was passed by the House on October 29, 2009, by a vote of 389-32, and referred to the Senate for consideration.[108] On November 2, 2009, the bill was referred to the Senate Committee on Small Business and Entrepreneurship.

The House committee report accompanying H.R. 3854 argued that "the existing licensing process is perhaps the single-greatest impairment to the SBIC program."[109] The report also indicated that the SBA's licensing procedures for experienced SBICs needed to be revised because the SBA's "licensing and relicensing process has become so cumbersome that many successful SBICs leave the program rather than deal with the arduous and lengthy task of SBA licensing."[110]

H.R. 5554, the Small Business Assistance and Relief Act of 2010, included the same legislative language contained in H.R. 3854 providing for expedited licensing procedures for experienced SBIC applicants.[111] It was introduced on June 17, 2010, and referred to the House Committee on Small Business.[112]

Legislation to Increase SBIC Financing Levels

In FY2010, the SBA's leverage ($931 million) amounted to less than one-third (31.0%) of its authorized level of $3 billion.[113] NASBIC has characterized the SBIC program as "dramatically underused."[114] It has argued that the program's financing levels would increase if (1) the SBA further improved its licensing processing procedures to make them more timely and objective, (2) the percentage of SBIC regulatory capital allowed from state or local government entities was increased from its present maximum of 33%, and (3) the SBIC program's family of funds limit (currently $225 million for two or more licenses under common control) was increased to allow SBICs to have a series of investment funds in place, where, for example, "one fund could be winding down, another could be at peak, and another could just be ramping up."[115]

H.R. 3854 and H.R. 5554 would have encouraged greater utilization of the SBIC program by increasing the maximum percentage of SBIC regulatory capital allowed from state or local government entities from 33% to 45%.[116] Both measures would have also increased the SBIC program's family of funds limit from $225 million to $350 million; increased the SBIC program's limit of $250 million to $400 million for multiple funds under common control who are licensed after September 30, 2009, and invest 50% of their dollars in low income geographic areas; and increased the SBIC program's authorization level from $3 billion to $5.5 billion in FY2011.[117]

Discussion

One of the SBA's goals is to enhance the SBIC program's "acceptance in the marketplace and increase the number of funds licensed and the amount of leverage issued so as to improve capital access for small businesses."[118] The SBA has asserted that ARRA's changes to the SBIC program will help it to achieve this goal. ARRA increased the maximum leverage available to SBICs to up "to three times the private capital raised by the SBIC, or $150 million, whichever is less, and $225 million for multiple licensees under common control" and increased "the maximum leverage amounts to $175 million for single funds and $250 million for multiple funds under common control who are licensed after September 30, 2009, and invest 50% of their dollars in low income geographic areas."[119] The SBA has not requested a further increase in the SBIC program's leverage limits or an increase in the program's current authorization level of $3 billion.

Advocates of increasing the SBIC program's leverage limits and authorization level to achieve a greater utilization of the SBIC program argue that these actions are necessary to help fill a gap "in the SBA's array of capital access programs."[120] For example, NASBIC has argued that the demise of the SBIC participating securities program and the current "underutilization" of the SBIC debentures program is preventing many small firms from accessing the capital necessary to fully realize their economic potential and assist in the national economic recovery.[121] Others worry about the potential risk an expanded SBIC program has for the taxpayer, especially if investments are targeted at startup and early-stage small businesses which, by definition, have a more limited credit history and a higher risk for default than businesses that have established positive cash flow.

CONCLUDING OBSERVATIONS

Some, including President Barack Obama, have agued that current economic conditions make it imperative that the SBA be provided additional resources to assist small businesses in acquiring capital necessary to start, continue, or expand operations and create jobs.[122] In their view, encouraging greater utilization of the SBIC program will increase small business access to capital, result in higher levels of job creation and retention, and promote economic growth. For example, the House Committee on Small Business report accompanying H.R. 3854 indicated that

> The SBA's lending and investment programs are intended to bridge the gap in financing that occurs when the private markets contract. Conventional wisdom would suggest that these programs would expand when the gap in private credit grows during times of economic stress. Unfortunately, that has not been the case in this economic

> downturn. A growing number of businesses have struggled to secure loans and other forms of capital through the SBA's lending and investment programs. Despite moderate improvements that can be attributed to the small business lending initiatives contained in ARRA, the conditions for small business credit have been slow to improve....
>
> If the declines in small business lending [are] to be halted, inherent deficiencies in the SBA's capital access programs must be addressed. The agency must have additional lending programs that are better suited to operate under conditions where lenders are under increased capital constraints and extremely sensitive to risk. Additionally, these programs must provide significant tangible benefits to small business borrowers that are struggling with lower revenues and greater uncertainty in the near-term. While the SBA's existing programs cannot meet these criteria, the changes implemented under H.R. 3854 [including enhancements to the SBIC program] will address these needs.[123]

Others worry about the potential risk an expanded SBIC program has for increasing the federal deficit. In their view, the best means to assist small business, promote economic growth, and create jobs is to reduce business taxes and exercise federal fiscal restraint.[124] For example, during floor debate on H.R. 3854 Representative Pete Sessions argued:

> This legislation ... would offer some assistance to small business, but I believe there are more effective ways to assist them during the economic crisis. For instance, not growing the size of government just to give them, small business, a loan. We should be doing things to improve small business by expensing, by permanently repealing the death tax, by extending tax relief, by improving regulatory reform, by not adding a cap-and-trade bill, and by ... not ... passing a health care bill which will diminish American jobs.[125]

As these quotations attest, congressional debate concerning the SBIC program has primarily involved assessments of the ability of small businesses to access capital from the private sector and evaluations of the program's risk, the effect of proposed changes on the program's risk, and the potential impact of the program's risk on the federal deficit. Empirical analysis of economic data can help inform debate concerning the ability of small businesses to access capital from the private sector and the extent of the program's risk, the affect of proposed changes on the program's risk, and the potential impact of the program's risk on the federal deficit. Additional data concerning SBIC investment impact on recipient job creation and firm survival might also prove useful. However, ultimately, these assessments are often secondary to personal value judgments concerning the federal government's role in promoting business, and the SBA's role in promoting small business.

APPENDIX. SMALL BUSINESS ELIGIBILITY REQUIREMENTS AND APPLICATION PROCESS

Small Business Eligibility Requirements

Only businesses that meet the SBA's definition of "small" may participate in the SBIC program. They must meet either the SBA's size standard for the industry in which they are primarily engaged, or a separate financial size standard which has been established for the SBIC program. SBICs use the size standard that is most likely to qualify the company, typically the financial size standard for the SBIC program. It is currently set as a maximum net worth of no more than $18 million and average after-tax net income for the preceding two years of not more than $6 million.[126] All of the company's subsidiaries, parent companies, and affiliates are considered in determining if it meets the size standard.

In addition, since 1997, the SBA has required SBICs to set aside a specified percentage of their financing to "businesses at the lower end of the permitted size range," primarily because "the financial size standards applicable to the SBIC program are considerably higher than those used in other SBA programs."[127] For example, P.L. 111-5, the American Recovery and Reinvestment Act of 2009 (ARRA), amended those regulations to require SBICs licensed on or after the date of its enactment (February 17, 2009) to certify that at least 25% of their future financing is invested in smaller enterprises. A smaller enterprise is a company that, together with any affiliates, either has net worth of no more than $6 million and average after-tax net income for the preceding two years of no more than $2 million, or meets the SBA's size standard in the industry in which the applicant is primarily engaged.[128]

SBICs licensed before February 17, 2009, that have not received any SBA leverage commitments after February 17, 2009, must have at least 20% of its aggregate financing dollars (plus 100% for leverage commitments over $90 million) invested in smaller enterprises.

SBICs licensed before February 17, 2009, that have received a SBA leverage commitment after February 17, 2009, must meet the 20% threshold (plus 100% for leverage commitments over $90 million) for financing provided before the date of the first leverage commitment issued after February 17, 2009, and the 25% threshold for financing made on or after such date.[129]

SBICs are not allowed to invest in the following: other SBICs; finance and investment companies or finance-type leasing companies; unimproved real estate; companies with less than 51% of their assets and employees in the United States; passive or casual businesses (those not engaged in a regular and continuous business operation); or companies that will use the proceeds to acquire farmland.[130] In addition, SBICs may not provide funds for a small business whose primary business activity is deemed contrary to the public interest or if the funds will be used substantially for a foreign operation.[131]

Small Business Application Process

Small business owners interested in receiving SBIC financing can search for active SBICs using the SBA's SBIC directory.[132] It provides contact information for all licensed SBICs, sorted by state. It also includes the SBIC's preferred minimum and maximum financing size range, the type of capital provided (e.g., equity, mezzanine, subordinated debt, 1st and 2nd lien secured term, and preferred stock), funding stage preference (e.g., early stage, growing and expansion stage, and later stage), industry preference (e.g., business services, manufacturing, environmental services, and distribution), geographic preference (e.g., national, regional, or specific state or states), and a description of the firm's focus (e.g., equity capital to later stage companies for expansion and acquisition, targeting companies with revenues of at least $5 million and profitability at the time of financing).[133]

After locating a suitable SBIC, the small business owner presents the SBIC a business plan that addresses the business's operations, management, financial condition, and funding requirements. The typical business plan includes the following information:

- the name of the business as it appears on the official records of the state or community in which it operates;

- the city, county, and state of the principal location and any branch offices or facilities;
- the form of business organization and, if a corporation, the date and state of incorporation;
- a description of the business, including the principal products sold or services rendered;
- a history of the general development of the products or services during the past five years (or since inception);
- information about the relative importance of each principal product or service to the volume of the business and to its profits;
- a description of business's real and physical property and adaptability to other business ventures;
- a description of technical attributes of its products and facilities;
- detailed information about the business's customer base, including potential customers;
- a marketing survey or economic feasibility study;
- a description of the distribution system for the business's products or services;
- a descriptive summary of the competitive conditions in the industry in which the business is engaged, including its competitive position relative to its largest and smallest competitors;
- a full explanation and summary of the business's pricing polices;
- brief resumes of the business's management personnel and principal owners, including their ages, education, and business experience;
- banking, business, and personal references for each member of management and for the principal owners;
- balance sheets and profit and loss statements for the last three fiscal years (or from inception);
- detailed projections of revenues, expenses, and net earnings for the coming year;
- a statement of the amount of funding requested and the time requirements for the funds;
- the reasons for the request for funds and a description of the proposed uses; and
- a description of the benefits the business expects to gain from the financing (e.g., expansion, improvement in financial position, expense reduction, and increase in efficiency).[134]

Because SBICs typically receive hundreds of business plans per year, the SBA recommends that small business owners seek a personal referral or introduction to the particular SBIC fund manager being targeted to increase "the likelihood that the business plan will be carefully considered."[135] According to NASBIC, "a thorough study an SBIC must undertake before it can make a final decision could take several weeks or longer."[136]

End Notes

[1] U.S. Small Business Administration, "Fiscal Year 2011 Congressional Budget Justification and FY2009 Annual Performance Report," Washington, DC, 2010, p. 1.

[2] 15 U.S.C. § 661.

[3] U.S. Congress, House Committee on Banking and Currency, *Small Business Investment Act of 1958*, report to accompany S.3651, 85th Cong., 2nd sess., June 30, 1958, H.Rept. 85-2060 (Washington: GPO, 1958), pp. 4, 5.

[4] Ibid., p. 5.

[5] P.L. 92-595, the Small Business Investment Act Amendments of 1972.

[6] 13 CFR § 107.50.

[7] Ibid.

[8] Commercial banks may invest up to 5% of their capital and surplus to partially or wholly own an SBIC. Bank investments in an SBIC are presumed by federal regulatory agencies to be a "qualified investment" for Community Reinvestment Act purposes. See P.L. 90-104, the Small Business Act Amendments of 1967; The Board of Governors of the Federal Reserve Board, "Small Business Investment Companies," 33 *Federal Register* 6967, May 9, 1968; and U.S. Small Business Administration, "Small Business Investment Companies (SBICs)," *Small Business Notes*, Washington, DC, 2009, http://www.smallbusinessnotes.com/financing/sbic.html.

[9] U.S. Small Business Administration, "For SBIC Applicants," Washington, DC, http://archive.sba.gov/aboutsba/sbaprograms/inv/forsbicapp/INV_APPLICATION_PROCESS.html.

[10] Ibid.

[11] 13 CFR § 107.210.

[12] Ibid.

[13] 13 CFR § 107.150.

[14] 13 CFR § 107.230.

[15] 13 CFR § 107.210.

[16] 13 CFR § 107.150.

[17] 13 CFR § 107.230.

[18] U.S. Small Business Administration, "SBIC Management Assessment Questionnaire and License Application: Form 2181," Washington, DC, p. 21, http://www.sba.gov/sites/default/files/inv_sba_form_2181.pdf.

[19] U.S. Small Business Administration, "For SBIC Applicants," Washington, DC, *http://archive.sba.gov/aboutsba/sbaprograms/inv/forsbicapp/INV_APPLICATION_PROCESS.html*; and U.S. Small Business Administration, Office of Legislative Affairs, correspondence with the authors, September 21, 2100.

[20] 13 CFR § 107.800. The SBIC is not allowed to become a general partner in any unincorporated business or become jointly or severally liable for any obligations of an unincorporated business.

[21] 13 CFR § 107.810; and 13 CFR § 107.840.

[22] 13 CFR § 107.815. Debt securities are instruments evidencing a loan with an option or any other right to acquire equity securities in a small business or its affiliates, or a loan which by its terms is convertible into an equity position, or a loan with a right to receive royalties that are excluded form the cost of money.

[23] 13 CFR § 107.820.

[24] 13 CFR § 107.730.

[25] 13 CFR § 107.865. The period of time that an SBIC can exercise control over a small business for purposes connected with its investment through ownership of voting securities, management agreements, voting trusts, majority representation on the board of directors, or otherwise, is "limited to the seventh anniversary of the date on which such control was initially acquired, or any earlier date specified by the terms of any investment agreement." With the SBA's prior written approval, an SBIC "may retain control for such additional period as may be reasonably necessary to complete divestiture of control or to ensure the financial stability of the portfolio company."

[26] A tier of SBA leverage equals the amount of the SBIC's private (regulatory) capital. SBICs approved for less than two tiers of SBA leverage must not invest more than 20% of its private capital in any one small business if the SBIC's plan contemplates one tier of leverage and no more than 25% of its private capital if its plan contemplates 1.5 tiers of leverage. See 13 CFR § 107.740; and U.S. Small Business Administration, "American Recovery and Investment Act of 2009: Implementation of SBIC Program Changes," letter from Harry Haskins, Acting Associate Administrator for Investment, to All Small Business Investment Companies (SBICs) and Applicants, Washington, DC, May 4, 2009, p. 2, http://archive.sba.gov/idc/groups/public/documents/sba_program_office/inv_rcvry_act_sbic _changes.pdf.

[27] 13 CFR § 107.720.

[28] Ibid.

[29] Ibid. SBICs may provide venture capital financing to "disadvantaged concerns" engaged in relending or reinvesting activities (except agricultural credit companies and banking and savings and loan institutions not insured by a federal agency). Without SBA approval, these financings, at the end of the fiscal year, may not exceed the SBIC's regulatory capital. A disadvantaged concern is defined as a small business that is at least 50% owned, controlled, and managed, on a day-to-day basis, by a person or persons whose participation in the free enterprise system is hampered because of social or economic disadvantages.

[30] The SBA has a general interest rate ceiling of 19% for a loan and 14% for a debt security, with provisions for a higher interest rate under specified circumstances. See 13 CFR § 107.855. SBICs are allowed to collect a nonrefundable application fee of no more than 1% of the amount of financing requested from a small business to review its financing application, a closing fee of no more than 2% of the amount of financing requested from a small business concern for a loan, charged no earlier than the date of the first disbursement, and a closing fee of no more than 4% of the amount of financing requested from a small business concern for a debt security or equity security financing, charged no earlier than the date of the first disbursement. SBICs are also allowed to charge a small business for reasonable out-of-pocket expenses, other than management expenses incurred to process the small business's financing application. See 13 CFR § 107.860.

[31] U.S. Small Business Administration, "Small Business Investment Companies," 64 *Federal Register* 52645, September 30, 1999.

[32] U.S. Small Business Administration, "Small Business Investment Companies," 64 *Federal Register* 52641-52646, September 30, 1999. LMIs Zones are areas located in a HUBZone, an Urban Empowerment Zone or Urban Enterprise Community designated by the Secretary of the U.S. Department of Housing and Urban Development, a Rural Empowerment Zone or Rural Enterprise Community as designated by the Secretary of the U.S. Department of Agriculture, an area of low income or moderate income as recognized by the Federal

Financial Institutions Examination Council, or a county with persistent poverty as classified by the U.S. Department of Agriculture's Economic Research Service. See 13 CFR § 107.50.

[33] U.S. Small Business Administration, "For SBICs: Background Information on Low or Moderate Income(LMI) Debentures," Washington, DC, http://archive.sba.gov/aboutsba/ sba programs/inv/forsbic/inv_backgroundinfo.html.

[34] U.S. Small Business Administration, "SBIC Program Financing to Small Businesses – Fiscal Year 2010: Summary of SBIC Program Financing," Washington, DC.

[35] 13 CFR § 107.1120; 13 CFR § 107.1150; and U.S. Small Business Administration, "American Recovery and Investment Act of 2009: Implementation of SBIC Program Changes," letter from Harry Haskins, Acting Associate Administrator for Investment, to All Small Business Investment Companies (SBICs) and Applicants, Washington, DC, May 4, 2009, p. 1, http://archive.sba.gov/idc/groups/public/documents/sba_program_office/ inv_rcvry_act_sbic_changes.pdf.

[36] 13 CFR § 107.1150.

[37] 13 CFR § 107.1100.

[38] The SBA is required by statute to issue guarantees "at periodic intervals of not less than every 12 months and shall do so at such shorter intervals as it deems appropriate, taking into consideration the amount and number of such guarantees or trust certificates." See 15 U.S.C. § 687m.

[39] U.S. Small Business Administration, "Offering Circular, Guaranteed 4.727% Participating Securities Participation Certificates, Series SBIC-PS 2009-10 A," Washington, DC, p. 11, http://www.sba.gov/idc/groups/public/documents/ sba_program_office/inv_sbic-ps-2009-10a-831641ep6.pdf.

[40] U.S. Small Business Administration, "Small Business Investment Companies (SBICs)," *Small Business Notes*, Washington, DC, 2009, http://www.smallbusinessnotes.com/financing/ sbic.html; and U.S. Small Business Administration, "For SBIC Applicants," Washington, DC, http://archive.sba.gov/aboutsba/sbaprograms/inv/forsbicapp/INV_APPLICATION _PROCESS.html.

[41] Ibid.; 13 CFR § 107.50; and 13 CFR § 107.1150.

[42] The coupon (interest) rate on SBA debentures is based on the 10-year Treasury rate (adjusted to the nearest 1/8th of one percent) plus a market-driven spread, currently about 70-80 basis points. See 13 CFR § 107.50; and U.S. Small Business Administration, "SBIC Program: FAQs," Washington, DC, http://archive.sba.gov/aboutsba/sbaprograms/inv/ faq/index.html. The coupon rate for the most recent sale of a SBA debenture participating certificate, which took place on March 24, 2010, was 4.108%. U.S. Small Business Administration, "Offering Circular, Guaranteed 4.108% Debenture Participation Certificates, Series SBIC 2010-10 A," Washington, DC, http://archive.sba.gov/idc/groups/ public/documents/sba_program_ office/inv_sbic-2010-10-a-831641es0.pdf.

[43] U.S. Congress, House Committee on Small Business, *Small Business Financing and Investment Act of 2009*, report to accompany H.R. 3854, 111th Cong., 1st sess., October 26, 2009, H.Rept. 111-315 (Washington: GPO, 2009), p. 11; and U.S. Small Business Administration, "SBIC Program: FAQs," Washington, DC, http://archive.sba.gov/aboutsba/ sbaprograms/inv/faq/index.html.

[44] 13 CFR § 107.1130; and 13 CFR § 107.1210.

[45] U.S. Congress, House Committee on Small Business, *Subcommittee Markup of Legislation Affecting the SBA Capital Access Programs*, 111th Cong., 1st sess., October 8, 2009, House Small Business Committee Document No. 111-050 (Washington: GPO, 2009), pp. 7, 10, 11, 187-194; U.S. Congress, House Committee on Small Business, *Full Committee Hearing on Increasing Capital for Small Business*, 111th Cong., 1st sess., October 14, 2009, House Small Business Committee Document No. 111-051 (Washington: GPO, 2009), pp. 1, 2, 40, 98; and U.S. Congress, House Committee on Small Business, *Small Business Financing and Investment Act of 2009*, report to accompany H.R. 3854, 111th Cong., 1st sess., October 26, 2009, H.Rept. 111-315 (Washington: GPO, 2009), pp. 3, 4, 10-12.

[46] 13 CFR § 107.1500; and U.S. Small Business Administration, "Offering Circular, Guaranteed 4.727% Participating Securities Participation Certificates, Series SBIC-PS 2009-10 A," Washington, DC, pp. 7, 14, http://archive.sba.gov/idc/groups/public/documents/sba _program_office/inv_sbic-ps-2009-10a-831641ep6.pdf.

[47] U.S. Small Business Administration, "Offering Circular, Guaranteed 4.727% Participating Securities Participation Certificates, Series SBIC-PS 2009-10 A," Washington, DC, p. 2, http://archive.sba.gov/idc/groups/public/documents/ sba_program_office/inv_sbic-ps-2009-10a-831641ep6.pdf.

[48] Ibid., pp. 2, 3. Also, see U.S. Congress, House Committee on Small Business, *Private Equity for Small Firms: The Importance of the Participating Securities Program*, 109th Cong., 1st sess., April 13, 2005, Serial No. 109-10 (Washington: GPO, 2005), p. 5.

[49] The coupon rate for most recent sale of a SBA guaranteed participating securities participation certificate, which took place on February 25, 2010, was 4.727%. U.S. Small Business Administration, "Offering Circular, Guaranteed 4.727% Participating Securities Participation Certificates, Series SBIC-PS 2009-10 A," Washington, DC, p. 1, http:// archive.sba. gov/idc/groups/public/documents/sba_program_office/inv_sbic-ps-2009-10a-831641ep6.pdf.

[50] U.S. Congress, House Committee on Small Business, *Small Business Financing and Investment Act of 2009*, report to accompany H.R. 3854, 111th Cong., 1st sess., October 26, 2009, H.Rept. 111-315 (Washington: GPO, 2009), p. 11; and U.S. Small Business Administration, "SBIC Program: FAQs," Washington, DC, http://archive.sba.gov/aboutsba/ sbaprograms/inv/faq/index.html.

[51] U.S. Congress, House Committee on Small Business, *Private Equity for Small Firms: The Importance of the Participating Securities Program*, 109th Cong., 1st sess., April 13, 2005, Serial No. 109-10 (Washington: GPO, 2005), p. 5, 33; and U.S. Small Business Administration, "SBIC Program: FAQs," Washington, DC, http://archive.sba.gov/about sba/sbaprograms/inv/faq/index.html.

[52] 13 CFR § 107.1500. SBICs that wish to be eligible to issue participating securities must have regulatory capital of at least $10 million unless it can demonstrate to the SBA's satisfaction that it can be financially viable over the long-term with a lower amount, but not less than $5 million. See 13 CFR § 107.210. They must also maintain sufficient liquidity to avoid a condition of "Liquidity Impairment," defined as a liquidity ratio (total current funds available divided by total current funds required) of less than 1.2. See 13 CFR § 107.1505. The only type of debt, other than leverage, SBICs that have applied to issue participating securities or have outstanding participating securities are permitted to incur is temporary debt. Temporary debt is defined as short-term borrowings from a regulated financial institution, a regulated credit company, or a non-regulated lender approved by the SBA for the purpose of maintaining the SBIC's operating liquidity or providing funds for a particular financing of a small business. The total outstanding borrowings, not including leverage, can not exceed 50% of the SBIC's leveraged capital and all such borrowings must be fully paid off for at least 30 consecutive days during the SBIC's fiscal year so that it has no outstanding third-party debt for 30 days. See 13 CFR § 107.570. SBICs issuing participating securities are required to invest an amount equal to the original issue price of such securities solely in equity capital investments (e.g., common or preferred stock, limited partnership interests, options, warrants, or similar equity instruments). See 13 CFR § 107.1505.

[53] U.S. Small Business Administration, "Offering Circular, Guaranteed 4.727% Participating Securities Participation Certificates, Series SBIC-PS 2009-10 A," Washington, DC, p. 7, http://archive.sba.gov/idc/groups/public/documents/ sba_program_office/inv_sbic-ps-2009-10a-831641ep6.pdf.

[54] U.S. Small Business Administration, Investment Division, "SBIC Program Overview," Washington, DC, June 3, 2011, p. 1, http://www.nasbic.org/resource/resmgr/ Docs/SBIC _Program_Stats June_3_20.pdf.

[55] 13 CFR § 107.630; and 13 CFR § 107.690.

[56] 13 CFR § 107.640.

[57] 13 CFR § 107.650.

[58] Ibid.

[59] 13 CFR § 107.660.

[60] U.S. Small Business Administration, Investment Division, "SBIC Program Overview," Washington, DC, June 3, 2011, p. 1, http://www.nasbic.org/resource/resmgr/Docs/SBIC_ Program_Stats_June_3_20.pdf.

[61] U.S. Small Business Administration, "SBIC Program Financing to Small Businesses – Fiscal Year 2010: Form of Business, Pre-Financing Information, and Licensing Activity Levels," Washington, DC.

[62] In recent years, the SBA has made it a goal to increase the number of new SBIC licenses issued each year. In FY2008, the SBA issued six new SBIC licenses (five to debenture SBICs and one to a bank-owned/non-leveraged SBIC). In FY2009, the SBA issued 11 new SBIC licenses (eight to debenture SBICs and three to bank-owned/non-leveraged SBICs). In FY2010, the SBA issued 23 new SBIC licenses (21 to debenture SBICs and 2 to bank-owned/non-leveraged SBICs). See U.S. Small Business Administration, Investment Division, "SBIC Program Overview," Washington, DC, October 13, 2010, p. 2, *http://www. nasbic.org/resource/resmgr/Docs/SBIC_Stats_Oct._13.pdf.*

[63] Ibid., p. 1.

[64] U.S. Small Business Administration, Press Office, "SBA Growth Capital Program Provides Record $1.59 Billion in Financing for Small Businesses in FY10," October 14, 2010, http://www.sba.gov/content/sba-growth-capital-program-provides-record-159-billion-financing-small-businesses-fy10; and U.S. Small Business Administration, "SBIC 2011-10 A, CUSIP 83164 EU5, Offering Circular," Washington, DC, http://www.sba.gov/ content/sbic-2011-10- cusip-831641-eu5-0. The SBA has a selected list of firms that have received SBIC financing, including Apple Computer, Compaq Computer, Costco Wholesale Corporation, FedEx, Intel, Jenny Craig, Inc., Outback Steakhouse, Sports Authority, Staples, and Sun Microsystems, on its website. See U.S. Small Business Administration, "Investment Division," Washington, DC, http://archive.sba.gov/aboutsba/ sbaprograms/inv/ INV_SUCCESS_STORIES.html.

[65] U.S. Small Business Administration, Investment Division, "SBIC Program Overview," Washington, DC, June 3, 2011, p. 1, http://www.nasbic.org/resource/resmgr/Docs/SBIC _Program_Stats_June_3_20.pdf.

[66] Ibid.

[67] U.S. Small Business Administration, "SBIC Program Financing to Small Businesses – Fiscal Year 2010: Summary of SBIC Program Financing," Washington, DC.

[68] U.S. Small Business Administration, "SBIC Program Financing to Small Businesses – Fiscal Year 2010: Use of Proceeds by the Financed Businesses," Washington, DC.

[69] U.S. Small Business Administration, Office of Legislative Affairs, correspondence with the author, October 20, 2010; U.S. Small Business Administration, "Fiscal Year 2011 Congressional Budget Justification and FY2009 Annual Performance Report," Washington, DC, 2010, pp. 19, 51; and U.S. Small Business Administration, "FY2010 Congressional Budget Justification," Washington, DC, 2009, pp. 17, 42.

[70] National Venture Capital Association, "Corporate VC Stats as of 12/31/2010 by Year," Arlington, VA, http://www.nvca.org/index.php?option=com_content&view=article&id=78: latest - industry-statistics&catid= 40:research&Itemid=102.

[71] U.S. Small Business Administration, "Fiscal Year 2011 Congressional Budget Justification and FY2009 Annual Performance Report," Washington, DC, 2010, p. 52.

[72] Kenneth Temkin and Brett Theodos, with Kerstin Gentsch, The Debenture Small Business Investment Company Program: A Comparative Analysis of Investment Patterns with Private Venture Capital Equity, The Urban Institute , Washington, DC, January 2008, p. 3, http://www.urban.org/UploadedPDF/411601_sbic_gap_analysis.pdf.

[73] Ibid., p. 1.

74 U.S. Small Business Administration, "SBIC Program Financing to Small Businesses – Fiscal Year 2010: Demographics of Financed Businesses," Washington, DC.

75 Kenneth Temkin and Brett Theodos, with Kerstin Gentsch, The Debenture Small Business Investment Company Program: A Comparative Analysis of Investment Patterns with Private Venture Capital Equity, The Urban Institute , Washington, DC, January 2008, pp. 2, 26, http://www.urban.org/UploadedPDF/411601_sbic_gap_analysis.pdf.

76 U.S. Congress, House Committee on Small Business, *Full Committee Hearing on Legislation Updating and Improving the SBA's Investment and Surety Bond Programs*, 110th Cong., 1st sess., September 6, 2007, Serial Number 110-44 (Washington: GPO, 2007), p. 15.

77 Ibid.

78 U.S. Congress, House Committee on Small Business, *Full Committee Hearing On Increasing Capital For Small Business*, 111th Cong., 1st sess., October 14, 2009, House Small Business Committee Document No. 111-051 (Washington: GPO, 2009), p. 89.

79 Kenneth Temkin and Brett Theodos, with Kerstin Gentsch, The Debenture Small Business Investment Company Program: A Comparative Analysis of Investment Patterns with Private Venture Capital Equity, The Urban Institute , Washington, DC, January 2008, pp. 3, 18-24, http://www.urban.org/UploadedPDF/411601_sbic_gap_analysis.pdf.

80 National Venture Capital Association, "Venture Capital Investments Q3-2010 – MoneyTree Results, Regional Data," Arlington, VA, October 15, 2010, p. 17, http://www.nvca.org/.

81 Kenneth Temkin and Brett Theodos, with Kerstin Gentsch, The Debenture Small Business Investment Company Program: A Comparative Analysis of Investment Patterns with Private Venture Capital Equity, The Urban Institute , Washington, DC, January 2008, pp. 3, 11-17, http://www.urban.org/UploadedPDF/411601_sbic_gap_analysis.pdf.

82 Ibid., p. 11.

83 13 CFR § 107.1120; 13 CFR § 107.1150; and U.S. Small Business Administration, "American Recovery and Investment Act of 2009: Implementation of SBIC Program Changes," letter from Harry Haskins, Acting Associate Administrator for Investment, to All Small Business Investment Companies (SBICs) and Applicants, Washington, DC, May 4, 2009, p. 1, http://archive.sba.gov/idc/groups/public/documents/sba_program_office/ inv_rcvry_act_sbic_changes.pdf.

84 13 CFR § 107.1150; and 13 CFR § 107.710.

85 13 CFR § 107.1150.

86 Representative Edward Perlmutter, "Providing for Further Consideration of H.R. 5297, Small Business Jobs and Credit Act of 2010, Roll No. 368," *Congressional Record*, daily edition, vol. 156, no. 91 (June 17, 2010), pp. H4608, H4609.

87 H.R. 5297, the Small Business Lending Fund Act of 2010, Sec. 399L. Definitions.

88 Ibid. The nine targeted industries are: agricultural technology, energy technology, environmental technology, life science, information technology, digital media, clean technology, defense technology, and photonics technology. A similar $200 million Small Business Early-Stage Investment Program was included in H.R. 3854, the Small Business Financing and Investment Act of 2009, which was passed by the House on October 29, 2009, by a vote of 389-32. It is awaiting action in the Senate.

89 Senator Al Franken, "Small Business Lending Fund Act of 2010," Rollcall Vote No. 237 Leg., *Congressional Record*, daily edition, vol. 156, part 125 (September 16, 2010), p. S7158.

90 P.L. 111-240, the Small Business Jobs Act of 2010, Sec. 1131. Small Business Intermediary Lending Pilot Program.

91 H.Rept. 111-315, to accompany H.R. 3854, the Small Business Financing and Investment Act of 2009, p. 2. For the arguments presented by various organizations advocating the program see U.S. Congress, House Committee on Small Business, *Subcommittee on Finance and Tax Hearing on Legislative Proposals to Reform the SBA's Capital Access Programs*, 111th Cong., 1st sess., July 23, 2009, House Small Business Committee Document No. 111-039 (Washington: GPO, 2009), pp. 10-12, 60-67; and U.S. Congress, House Committee on Small Business, *Full Committee Hearing on Increasing Access to Capital for Small*

[91] *Business*, 111th Cong., 1st sess., October 14, 2009, House Small Business Committee Document No. 111-051 (Washington: GPO, 2009), pp. 33-35, 50-54, 63-69, 86-99.

[92] H.Rept. 111-315, to accompany H.R. 3854, the Small Business Financing and Investment Act of 2009, p. 3.

[93] Ibid., p. 20.

[94] Representative Sam Graves, "Small Business Jobs and Credit Act of 2010," House debate, *Congressional Record*, vol. 156, no. 90 (June 16, 2010), p. H4516.

[95] Ibid; and Representative Jeff Flake, "Small Business Early-Stage Investment Act of 2009," House debate, *Congressional Record*, vol. 155, no. 171 (November 18, 2009), p. H13083.

[96] U.S. Small Business Administration, Office of the Inspector General, "FY2003 Agency Management Challenges," Washington, DC, January 17, 2003, p. 30, *http://archive.sba.gov/ ig/onlinelibrary/tmc/index.html*.

[97] U.S. Small Business Administration, Office of the Inspector General, "FY2005 Report on the Most Serious Management and Performance Challenges Facing the SBA," Washington, DC, October 15, 2004, p. 11, http://archive.sba.gov/idc/groups/public/documents/ sba/oig_ reports_tmc_fy05.pdf.

[98] U.S. Small Business Administration, Office of the Inspector General, "FY2005 Report on the Most Serious Management and Performance Challenges Facing the SBA," Washington, DC, October 15, 2004, p. 11, http://archive.sba.gov/idc/groups/public/documents/sba/ oig_reports_tmc_fy05.pdf.

[99] The most recent Office of the Inspector General's annual reports on the most serious management and performance challenges facing the SBA are on-line at http://www.sba.gov/office-of-inspector-general/875 and an archive of reports since FY2000 can be viewed at http://archive.sba.gov/ig/onlinelibrary/tmc/index.html.

[100] U.S. Small Business Administration, Office of the Inspector General, "FY2010 Report on the Most Serious Management and Performance Challenges Facing the SBA," Washington, DC, October 16, 2009, p. 7, http://www.sba.gov/office-of-inspector-general/875/12354.

[101] U.S. Small Business Administration, Office of the Inspector General, "FY2011 Report on the Most Serious Management and Performance Challenges Facing the SBA," Washington, DC, October 15, 2010, p. 10, http://www.sba.gov/sites/default/files/oig_reports_tmc_fy 11_0.pdf.

[102] U.S. Small Business Administration, "FY2011 Congressional Budget Justification and FY2009 Annual Performance Report," Washington, DC, 2010, p. 51; and U.S. Congress, House Committee on Small Business, *Full Committee Hearing on Increasing Access to Capital for Small Businesses*, 111th Cong., 1st sess., October 14, 2009, House Small Business Committee Document No. 111-051 (Washington: GPO, 2009), p. 88.

[103] U.S. Small Business Administration, Office of Legislative Affairs, correspondence with the authors, September 21, 2100.

[104] U.S. Congress, House Committee on Small Business, *Full Committee Hearing on Laying the Groundwork for Economic Recovery: Expanding Small Business Access to Capital*, 111th Cong., 1st sess., June 10, 2009, House Committee on Small Business Document No. 111-028 (Washington: GPO, 2009), pp. 10, 22, 23, 70.

[105] U.S. Small Business Administration, Office of Legislative Affairs, correspondence with the authors, September 21, 2100.

[106] Ibid.

[107] The bill defines good standing as being a licensed leveraged or non-leveraged SBIC actively operating on the date of the initial receipt of the application, having no principal manager found liable in a civil action for fraud if the SBA makes a reasonable determination based on evidence that such liability has a material adverse effect on the applicant's ability to perform required obligations required by a license, and having no principal manager under investigation by a governmental agency or authority, under indictment, or convicted of a felony for a violation of federal or state securities laws, fraud, or another criminal violation if such investigation, indictment, or conviction has a material adverse effect on the

applicant's ability to perform obligations required by a license. See H.R. 3854, the Small Business Financing and Investment Act of 2009, Sec. 402. Expedited Licensing for Experienced Applicants.

[108] Representative Diana DeGette, "Roll No. 830," House vote on H.R. 3854, *Congressional Record*, daily edition, vol. 155, part 159 (October 29, 2009), pp. H12116, H12117.

[109] U.S. Congress, House Committee on Small Business, *Small Business Financing and Investment Act of 2009*, report to accompany H.R. 3854, 111th Cong., 1st sess., October 26, 2009, H.Rept. 111-315 (Washington: GPO, 2009), p. 36.

[110] Ibid.

[111] H.R. 5554, the Small Business Assistance and Relief Act of 2010, Sec. 592. Expedited Licensing for Experienced Applicants.

[112] The bill was also referred to the House Committees on Ways and Means, Appropriations, Energy and Commerce, and Financial Services, for a period to be subsequently determined by the Speaker, in each case for consideration of such provisions as fall within the jurisdiction of the committee concerned.

[113] U.S. Small Business Administration, Office of Legislative Affairs, correspondence with the author, October 20, 2010.

[114] U.S. Congress, House Committee on Small Business, *Full Committee Hearing On Increasing Capital For Small Business*, 111th Cong., 1st sess., October 14, 2009, House Small Business Committee Document No. 111-051 (Washington: GPO, 2009), pp. 32, 87.

[115] U.S. Congress, House Committee on Small Business, *Full Committee Hearing On Increasing Capital For Small Business*, 111th Cong., 1st sess., October 14, 2009, House Small Business Committee Document No. 111-051 (Washington: GPO, 2009), pp. 88, 89.

[116] H.R. 3854, the Small Business Financing and Investment Act of 2009, Sec. 401. Increased Investment from States; and H.R. 5554, the Small Business Assistance and Relief Act of 2010, Sec. 591. Increased Investment from States.

[117] H.R. 3854, the Small Business Financing and Investment Act of 2009, Sec. 401. Increased Investment From States, Sec. 403. Revised Leverage Limitations For Successful SBICs, and Sec. 408. Program Levels; and H.R. 5554, the Small Business Assistance and Relief Act of 2010, Sec. 591. Increased Investment from States, Sec. 593. Revised Leverage Limitations for Successful SBICs, and Sec. 598. Program Levels.

[118] U.S. Small Business Administration, "Fiscal Year 2011 Congressional Budget Justification and FY2009 Annual Performance Report," Washington, DC, 2010, p. 52.

[119] U.S. Small Business Administration, "SBA Project Plan, Section 505: SBIC Program Changes," Washington, DC, June 16, 2010, http://archive.sba.gov/idc/groups/public/documents/sba_homepage/sba_sbic_plan.pdf.

[120] U.S. Congress, House Committee on Small Business, *Small Business Financing and Investment Act of 2009*, report to accompany H.R. 3854, 111th Cong., 1st sess., October 26, 2009, H.Rept. 111-315 (Washington: GPO, 2009), p. 3.

[121] U.S. Congress, House Committee on Small Business, *Full Committee Hearing on Increasing Capital for Small Business*, 111th Cong., 1st sess., October 14, 2009, House Small Business Committee Document No. 111-051 (Washington: GPO, 2009), pp. 88-91.

[122] Representative Nydia Velázquez, "Small Business Financing and Investment Act of 2009," House debate, *Congressional Record*, daily edition, vol. 155, no. 159 (October 29, 2009), pp. H12074, H12075; Senator Mary Landrieu, "Statements on Introduced Bills and Joint Resolutions," remarks in the Senate, *Congressional Record*, daily edition, vol. 155, no. 185 (December 10, 2009), p. S12910; and The White House, "Remarks by the President on Job Creation and Economic Growth," Washington, DC, December 8, 2009, http://www.whitehouse.gov/the-press-office/ remarks-president-job-creation-and-economic-growth.

[123] U.S. Congress, House Committee on Small Business, *Small Business Financing and Investment Act of 2009*, committee print, 111th Cong., 1st sess., October 26, 2009, H.Rept. 111-315 (Washington: GPO, 2009), p. 5.

[124] National Federation of Independent Business, "Payroll Tax Holiday," Washington, DC, http://www.nfib.com/issues-elections/issues-elections-item/cmsid/49039/; and NFIB, "Government Spending," Washington, DC, http://www.nfib.com/issues-elections/issues-elections-item/cmsid/49051/.

[125] Representative Pete Sessions, "Providing for Consideration of H.R. 3854, Small Business Financing and Investment Act of 2009," House debate, *Congressional Record*, daily edition, vol. 155, part 159 (October 29, 2009), p. H12071.

[126] 13 CFR § 107.700; 13 CFR § 107.710; 13 CFR § 301(c)(2); and 13 CFR § 301(c)(1).

[127] U.S. Small Business Administration, "Small Business Investment Companies — Leverage Eligibility and Portfolio Diversification Requirements," 74 *Federal Register* 33912, July 14, 2009.

[128] 13 CFR § 107.710.

[129] U.S. Small Business Administration, "Small Business Investment Companies — Leverage Eligibility and Portfolio Diversification Requirements," 74 *Federal Register* 33912, July 14, 2009.

[130] 13 CFR § 107.720.

[131] Ibid.

[132] U.S. Small Business Administration, "Small Business Investment Companies: Entrepreneurs Seeking Financing," Washington, DC, http://archive.sba.gov/aboutsba/sbaprograms/inv/esf/INV_DIRECTORY_SBIC.html.

[133] Ibid.

[134] National Association of Small Business Investment Companies, "SBIC Financing: Step-by-Step," Washington, DC, http://www.nasbic.org/?page=SBIC_financing.

[135] U.S. Small Business Administration, "Small Business Investment Companies: Entrepreneurs Seeking Financing," Washington, DC, http://archive.sba.gov/aboutsba/sbaprograms/inv/esf/INV_DIRECTORY_SBIC.html.

[136] National Association of Small Business Investment Companies, "SBIC Financing: Step-by-Step," Washington, DC, http://www.nasbic.org/?page=SBIC_financing.

CHAPTER SOURCES

Chapter 1 - This is an edited, reformatted and augmented version of a Congressional Research Service publication, R41352, dated April 19th, 2011.

Chapter 2 - This is an edited, reformatted and augmented version of a U.S. Department of Justice publication R41456, dated June 23rd, 2011.

INDEX